Laws of the Jungle
Surviving Football's Monkey Business

Brian Laws with Alan Biggs

Best wishes

[signature]

Laws of the Jungle
Surviving Football's Monkey Business

Brian Laws with Alan Biggs

Vertical Editions
www.verticaleditions.com

First published in the United Kingdom in 2012 by Vertical Editions,
Unit 4a, Snaygill Industrial Estate, Skipton, North Yorkshire
BD23 2QR

www.verticaleditions.com

ISBN 978-1-904091-67-7

A CIP catalogue record for this book is available from the
British Library

Cover design by HBA, York

Printed and bound by MPG, Bodmin

To my ever-loving family. I've done this book for them and I couldn't have done it without them. So big thanks to my wife, Jane, and children Jaimie, Danielle and Thomas for their love and support. I wanted to leave a record of my eventful life in football that would last for ever. Something to hand down to my grandchildren and their children. It might also show them what a plonker I've been at times but, hey, nobody's perfect!

Contents

Contents

Acknowledgments

Co-author Alan Biggs and myself have had such long chats in the cause of writing this book that after the first session – at a motorway service station – both of us picked up fines for staying over the limit in the car park! We're now hoping the royalties cover it! And I'd like to thank Alan for his journalistic expertise, which proved a good deal better than his timekeeping!

When Alan first approached me with the book proposal, it sparked back to life an idea I'd had a few years earlier. And in that respect, I must also thank Scunthorpe journalist Bob Steels for laying down some of the groundwork for this project.

Last but not least, a big thanks to Karl Waddicor of publishers Vertical Editions for recognising this work as the masterpiece it is! Well, we can all dream, can't we? That, after all, is what a life in football is all about . . .

Prologue

Brian Laws has played in all four professional divisions of English football. He has also managed at every level. And he spent six years playing under the most charismatic manager the English game has ever seen, the legendary Brian Clough.

Yet even Cloughie was never at the centre of a bigger sensation than the day Laws, as a young manager in his first job, was embroiled in a dressing room bust-up that left his star striker with a broken cheekbone.

Here, for the first time, Brian lifts the lid on his six years with Cloughie – and reveals what really happened on the night a certain Italian striker called Ivano Bonetti ended up in hospital, leaving his boss ambushed at home under siege from the media.

It has never emerged, either – until now – that Laws also engaged in a bout of fisticuffs with one of Nottingham Forest's top stars of the Clough era. And got thanked by his boss for hitting the player concerned! Life in a football dressing room is never dull; they were fun times for Laws at the City Ground.

However, there are also chilling reflections on being a Nottingham Forest player on the day of the Hillsborough Disaster. And of the replay anguish that left him the victim of a cruel put-down by John Aldridge, a star on whom Laws was later to exact a type of revenge – using Bonetti as bait!

In between times, Laws has been a Wembley winner,

fulfilling all the boyhood dreams he nurtured at the famous Wallsend Boys Club. But above all, this is the story of a life in football and how to survive in it. His journey takes us through Burnley, Huddersfield, Middlesbrough, Nottingham, Grimsby, Scunthorpe, Sheffield and Burnley again.

Along the way, Brian has endured career-threatening injuries, managerial bust-ups and, inevitably, being sacked. But there have been plenty of laughs and, besides, he has repeatedly bounced back into the fray. Why? Because, having grown up in the soccer hotbed of the North East, he loves a game that has always been at the centre of his soul.

Brian is not, and would never claim to be, one of the biggest names. But this is one big read for anyone who shares his passion for football.

1

Strife of Brian: Having to Look on the Bright Side of Life

When I heard the voice on the other end of the phone I stood up, as if to attention. It was an instinctive reaction, a mark of respect. It was Brian Clough! "Young man, do you want to play for me?" – or words to that effect. Asking ME to play for HIM. Silly question. I'd have walked all the way from Middlesbrough to Nottingham over broken glass to do that!

This was 1988. Before and since the unforgettable day I signed for a legend at Forest, I have played for seven clubs and managed five. One in particular has seemed destined to remain missing from the list – my hometown favourites Newcastle United. Cloughie might have had an incredible aura around him and still does eight years after his death. But back in my boyhood days, the man who had me standing to attention was Malcolm Macdonald. Literally, that is. Standing with your feet barely touching the concrete floor on the seething, swaying terraces of St James' Park.

I worshipped at Supermac's feet. What feet they were,

too! And I had a dream of somehow filling his boots. Some chance, as it turned out! But like so many young kids, I wanted to be a striker – or a centre forward, as we still called them in those days. I was the "Supermac" of the famous Wallsend Boys Club for a couple of seasons, scoring loads of goals and winning lots of trophies. As an England international and the hero of the Toon Army, Malcolm was my idol. I liked to think there were similarities between us. He had bandy legs, I had bandy legs. He scored lots of goals, I scored lots of goals.

From the terraces at St James' Park I would watch his every move, standing with my mates at all Newcastle home games. To travel up from my home in Wallsend and see a mass of people dressed in black and white all heading in the same direction, it was a fantastic spectacle. You got sucked into the atmosphere. People used to be packed into the ground an hour before the start just to be sure of their place. It was brilliant being packed into those swaying masses. And even on a bitterly cold day, it was boiling hot in the middle of that lot. Now my reflections on those scenes are tinged with sadness as well as nostalgia, having been a player at Hillsborough on the day of the biggest disaster in British football. That is a story for a later chapter. For now, I am setting the scene on what it was like to be a kid with a dream growing up in the soccer hotbed of the North East. Other than a loving family – and you can't put a price on that – I had precious little else.

I was born in the shadow of the north Tyneside shipyards in Wallsend on October 14th, 1961 . . . the youngest of three children, with an older brother, John and a sister, Maureen. It was a really deprived area, right next to the shipyards where my father, Bob, worked. My first home in

Stuart's Terrace was exactly as it sounds – a small terraced house with just two bedrooms. It meant my brother and sister had to share, with a "pee" bucket in the middle of the room so we didn't have to go outside in winter. Believe me, that was brass monkey time. No central heating, of course, and no such thing as a bathroom, either, just the usual outside toilet.

All we had was a small tin bath which used to be hung up on the wall outside. When it was brought in to be placed in front of the fire it was always ice cold. So the water we poured in, however hot, used to cool very quickly. We'd fill the bath with canisters of hot water from the kettle and it seemed to take forever before there was enough for us to get in. I remember once, when I was about four or five, the bath was getting a bit rusty and my father daubed it blue with some paint he'd brought home from the shipyard. It was my turn to have first dip in the newly painted bath. The paint started to come off because of the hot water and I became blue from head to toe. I cried my eyes out but all my dad could do was laugh because it looked so funny to him. He was a strong character – you had to be to live in Wallsend in those days. I could twist my mum round my little finger but I knew that I could only go so far with my dad before he clamped down. He was a man of strong principles.

When I overstepped the mark I had some good hidings but I am sure I probably deserved them. They certainly did not do me any harm and I had great respect for my dad. It used to put the fear of God in me when Mum used to threaten she would tell him about something or other I was doing wrong. We lived right next to a main railway line and, like all young kids, me and my mates were attracted to it. Apart from watching the trains go by, there was a gap in the fence that we could get through. One week there was a fatality when a young boy was killed after straying on to the lines. But despite the warnings that were drummed into us, it was only a few days before we were back again. Somebody told my dad who had only just got back from work. He was knackered, had kicked off his shoes and was resting in front of the fire. But after the knock on the door he shot straight out of the house without even bothering to put his shoes on. He ran right across this derelict area that was covered with glass and rubble. Dad came through the gap in the fence and called me to him with the gentlest voice I have ever heard in my life. "Brian, come on down, your tea's ready." When I reached him he put his hand out – and my feet never touched the floor until we were back home. Every step my dad walked, he was almost crying with pain because his feet were cut to pieces. But it was painful for me, too – smack, smack, smack and "don't you ever go on there again!"

Wallsend was a deprived area and you had to be tough to survive. The weakest just got trod on. You had to stand up for yourself. It makes me wonder what would have happened to me if I had not become a professional footballer. I took a trip down memory lane recently and went back to the area where I grew up. But the houses are no more. They have long since been knocked down – and replaced by, of all things, a sewage farm! The one thing that lifted Wallsend and the whole of the North East was its football. Strangely enough, there was no football history in my family and Dad had little interest in the game. But from my earliest days all I ever wanted to be was a footballer. I lived and breathed the game, playing at every opportunity I got.

At school, I was forever kicking a ball around, much to the frustration of my teachers. Once I was punished for it in front of the whole school. They took my shoes off me so that I couldn't play and I was so distraught that I ran home to my mum in bare feet. Looking back, I must have been a right sod at school. I had no interest in the academic side, came away with nothing and I regret it now. I have had to do a lot of my own learning by going back to college or university and studying on my own. But I certainly wouldn't swap the life I've had in football.

It was at Wallsend Junior School that I took part in my first ever organised game. Mum and Dad could not afford to buy me boots so it was my brother John – who had just started working – who bought me my first pair. That's because he was so proud of me getting picked to play for the school team. Maybe I didn't appreciate it fully at the time, but John was always the one who pushed me towards my career and I'm so grateful to him for that.

By this time we had moved to a block of flats in another part of Wallsend – right next to a motorway and, more importantly, a big area of grass. It was our "Wembley." John always wanted to be a footballer, too – but he was useless! Always accident prone, he started as a goalkeeper and broke his arm making a save. But he loves the game and became a referee at local league level. In fact, he also did some scouting for me when I was manager of Scunthorpe and found a kid called Cliff Byrne who became a key defender for me. Anyway, after realising he would never be a player, John became a manager and ran his own team in the local Sunday league, appropriately called Battle Hill. John put me up front and I scored 60-odd goals in my first season. One of the teams we played against was Whitley Bay who were then managed by David Laws – no relation – who later became a Football League referee. Maybe because of the name, he hated our guts. But every time we played them I would score three or four. I was still only a kid playing against older lads but they would try to crock me and do anything to beat us. We can laugh about it now, although there were some real run-ins.

It was against David's team that I once embarrassed my brother so much that he wanted to disown me. For once we were losing and I was sulking because my team was rubbish and I couldn't get the ball. So I really spat my dummy out and just sat down in the middle of the pitch. John screamed at me to stand up but I just shouted back "no, no, I'm not." What a little git I must have been!

Despite that, it was around this time that Wallsend Boys Club took an interest in me. Basically, it was a club formed to keep boys off the street and try to give them some purpose in life. Their teams used to win everything right through from 11s to 16s. It was in training with them that I first learned the need to be disciplined. Everything about the club was so professional. They don't have a problem with any lad. If they do then that lad doesn't play for them again. Simple as that. You had to clean your boots, keep your shirt tucked in at all times and have your socks pulled up. Or have them pulled up for you!

Wallsend Boys Club's inspiration was a man named David Beardall who was in charge for about 30 years. During his stewardship, the club produced many young footballers who went on to play professionally. In my time, there were the likes of Steve Bruce and Peter Beardsley. Before that, Ray Hankin and two goalkeepers,

David Lawson and Eric Steele. And in more recent times, Lee Clark, Alan Thompson, Steve Watson and Michael Carrick. But the biggest name of all to have emerged from Wallsend was, of course, Alan Shearer. Enough said.

Wallsend had such a great reputation that I knew that if I played well for them I had a chance of attracting professional clubs. Being a Geordie, my natural dream was to wear the number 9 shirt of Newcastle United just like Malcolm Macdonald. But Wallsend had a coach called Peter Kirkley who just happened to be a scout for Burnley. In the school holidays he would take up to 30 kids to play on the training ground at Turf Moor. I was among the lucky ones to be asked back for more. And there were also invitations from Leicester, Coventry and West Brom.

By this time I was at Burnside Senior School in Wallsend where the highlight of my stay was a cameo appearance in a kids programme on Tyne Tees television called *The Paper Lads*. My school was asked to provide youngsters to take part in football scenes for one of the episodes. I was put forward and we had two days off school into the bargain. It was great diving around scoring with diving headers. When they put the programme together I was featured in three different scenes but only for a split second. Blink and you'd have missed me.

Another reality check was Burnside School saying that if I didn't knuckle down to my work they would refuse me permission to take up some of the invitations I'd had for professional trials. They also threatened to ban me from the school. Idle threats? Well, one day I got into real trouble. You could say it kind of "snowballed" – as you'll hear. The man caught in the avalanche was a Mr Calder, the technical drawing teacher and a great guy who also ran the school team. He knew how to get the best out of me in lessons, realised I liked doing things with my hands and put me on a course doing metalwork, woodwork – and bricklaying! I was bloody good at that. I enjoyed it, too, and if I hadn't been a footballer I'd have probably ended up a brickie. In fact, I still do bits of brickwork at home. I'm handy that way, keen on DIY when I've got the time. And I've spent that much money in B&Q I should be a shareholder in the company!

Anyway, it all went pear-shaped for Mr Calder and me when we were getting changed after one school match. He left this door open and, of course, the team were inquisitive. We found the room inside was like an Aladdin's Cave, full of sweets from the tuck shop. There were about 200 of these snowballs and after starting by trying to eat through them we just started splattering each other. There was cream everywhere. My best mate Jimmy Beresford started it all off but I ended up paying for it. The teacher went ballistic and banned me from playing football for a month. It was the hardest punishment he could have given. I'd have gladly taken a caning instead. I was supposed to go on trial to Coventry. They'd written a letter to the school asking for my release but now the headmaster refused.

I was just a nuisance at school, preferring to lark around. But when they stopped me going to Coventry I began to realise for the first time that I was jeopardising my dreams and needed to smarten up. My mum and dad went mad – I had let them down. And my brother, too, because he'd been spending a lot on my boots. He'd bought me a pair like George Best had at the time, with laces down the sides. What a top bro. At home, too, I was a pain in the arse. There was a block of garages and each "team" had a different door as their goal. Neighbours would come knocking to say: "Your Brian's smashed one of our windows again." It happened so many times that Dad used to cut a supply of wood in the shape of window frames and keep them in the cupboard so that he could go straight round to board up the ones I broke.

Finally, as my school days neared an end, came the offer I had dreamed about. A letter arrived for my parents inviting their son to Newcastle United for a trial. I was so excited – and yet it turned into a big disappointment.

I'd always been told when I went for a trial to have a good look at the first team and see if the club had a tradition of giving a chance to youngsters. There was me thinking I'd walk over broken glass if Newcastle asked me to sign for them. And they did. But my training with them was done in a car park and when one young lad was hurt going over on his ankle they just sent him off home without any treatment. In fact, he had broken his ankle. That made me turn the other way. I know it was only one little incident but it was enough to put me off the club that had always been an inspiration to me.

I decided to look in other directions and it was Burnley I found looming large on the horizon. They were traditionally a selling club but that was no bad thing for kids like me. Their first team at that time included six Geordies, of whom several were youngsters. Burnley had a reputation for picking up and developing talent. I thought this was my best chance to make the grade and that's exactly what happened – though not without a few traumas along the way.

2

Hello Burnley, Bye-bye Supermac

Best pal Jimmy Beresford did me a favour by starting that school bust-up over the sweets. Things really did "snowball" from there. For a start, it brought me to my senses. And Jimmy did me far more good than harm in other ways, too. Like me, he was up for anything and he also longed to be a professional footballer. Unfortunately, he could not quite make the grade. But that never stopped him being very supportive to me. It would have been easy for him to be jealous. Instead, Jimmy backed me all the way and I will never forget that. He went on to land a top job with the DHSS – so who knows, in today's precarious world of football management I could need another favour again some time!

I finished my exams at Burnside School on one day and went straight to Turf Moor the next. I was so excited I just threw my school uniform in the bin. And I never bothered to check my results; I've no idea of them even now. All I was interested in was one small bit of geography – finding my way from the heavy industrial heartland of the North East to the mill areas of East Lancashire. It was July 1977 and I was signing as an apprentice for Burnley at the age of 16. They were a club with a proud history – Football League champions in 1960, runners-up two years later when they were also FA Cup finalists, competitors in European competition. They had an unbroken spell in the old First Division from 1947 to 1971 but were in the Second when I arrived. The manager was Harry Potts, who had returned to the club after being the inspiration for some of their most successful years.

For all the excitement, I quickly became homesick. It was all very emotional, leaving home for the first time and saying goodbye to my mates as they all went off in different directions. It was heart-wrenching to be away. Every weekend I wanted to go home to my family and friends. But it's a fact of life that when you are chasing your dreams you have to travel. And I think that makes you more respectful of people and instils a greater desire to achieve. Once I had made the decision to join Burnley, I was determined to stick with it. That has been a trait I have followed wherever I have been as a player or manager. Call me stubborn, I suppose. Once my mind is made up, you can try to drag me any way you like, but I will always follow the direction I thought was right in the first place.

I believed Burnley was the right place to be, going there as a young striker. Let's not forget, though, that it was a different world for young kids trying to carve out a football career in those days. Life as an apprentice was so, so hard. The hours that a junior had to put in far exceeded the demands on senior players. Besides their own training, the youngsters had loads of chores to do. I had come from doing very little other than being at school and playing for kicks. So I quickly became physically and mentally exhausted. In fact, it was the most tired I have ever felt.

And it took me months to get used to this schedule. All I ever wanted to do when I got back to my digs at night was to go to bed and rest.

There were about 10 of us apprentices at Burnley and often our first job on a Monday morning was to sweep the terraces after the previous Saturday's game. The amount of stuff dropped on the floor and left behind by the fans was amazing. We used to find wallets and sometimes the odd fiver that had dropped out of someone's pocket. So the work had its compensations! Your head was always down, wondering what you were going to find next. But we hated it if it was a windy day because then we would often have to start all over again, brushing the terraces from top to bottom. On days like that the job seemed to take forever.

One day in particular I will never forget. Suddenly I heard a loud crack from above where I was working. I looked up to see that a hole had appeared in the roofing on top of the stand. And to my horror, falling through it was a workman who had been carrying out some repairs. He wasn't wearing a safety harness and he plunged down like some rag doll. His body crashed from one giant roof girder to another before smacking on to the concrete terracing below. It was a huge drop and he landed very close to us. Somehow he was still alive, but there was blood everywhere and a huge gap in his forehead. He even tried to get up, but couldn't. Everybody was in shock, but one of the lads ran to get the club physio while the rest of us did our best to comfort the man. He was still breathing but really he had "gone" and despite all the best work of the paramedics, he died in the ambulance on the way to hospital.

Away from the ground, I was living in digs. In fact, I must have stayed in eight different places during my early days at Burnley. That's a lot. And a lot too many for a young player trying to settle away from home for the first time. Acclimatising to a new life is one of the hardest challenges facing a youngster in football. The suitability of digs is vital for anyone who has uprooted his life at an early age. For me, circumstances made it a very difficult transition. The first place I stayed was near the training ground and it was like a hostel more than anything else with young police cadets living there, too. I couldn't settle and eventually went to see the manager. I was miserable as the only young player there and felt it was important to say something about not being in a football environment. It proved to be the first of several moves as I struggled to find somewhere permanent. I landed in some fairly peculiar places with some oddball characters and it was a while before I felt comfortable anywhere.

By the time I was a second-year apprentice at Burnley, I was getting fed up of having to wait for trains whenever I had the chance to go home to Newcastle. But it took me three attempts to pass my driving test. At the end of the first, I sat smugly at the wheel expecting the examiner to tell me I had passed. But I was rudely awakened. "I am failing you for driving too wide when overtaking a parked car," he said. I went: "What? Is that it?" I couldn't believe I'd done anything wrong. But he said: "Mr. Laws, you've failed – will you please leave the vehicle." I could have strangled him! My instructor told me to put in for a second test straightaway. It came six weeks later – with the same examiner who had failed me! My heart sank, but he assured me everything would be alright, just to remember what I had done wrong the first time.

So off we went and once more I thought I had done really well. Just a few questions about the highway code and that would be it. Then came the verdict: "I'm sorry, Mr. Laws, you've failed!" I demanded: "What for this time?" He replied: "You went over the line and cut it too sharp when taking a right hand turn."

I was gobsmacked. My brother came up with the answer. He suggested I should take the test somewhere else and got me booked in close to home at Bedlington where he used to live. First, I had to have a couple of lessons and I showed my instructor the documents stating why I had failed the first two tests. "You'd never have failed for that up here," he said. Sure enough, I passed. It was that easy.

Buying a car was the next struggle. On £17 a week, it was a problem. Once again brother John came to the rescue, taking out a £400 loan under his name on condition that I paid him back a tenner each week. That left me only £7 to live on, but I was so excited at the prospect of owning a car that I jumped at the offer. And I never let John down with the payments. I bought a K registered green Avenger – not really my choice of colour but at a price I could now afford. I thought it was the mint, just fantastic. And, besides enabling me to get home every weekend, I found a way of balancing the books. We had a lot of young guys from the North East at Burnley. I'd offer to drop them off wherever – but it was going to cost them! A bit of the manager in me coming out early, because I even made a small profit. Then, as I moved up the car market, I sold the Avenger to best mate Jimmy for £250. And it collapsed on him a few weeks later, needing a new gearbox, clutch, engine, the works! The moral of the story is . . . never sell a car to a friend.

Meanwhile, I was about to become a reconditioned footballer. In my second season as a Burnley apprentice I suffered an injury that changed the course of my career. It happened on the training ground, playing in my usual position up front. I was never scared of the physical side and would always be brave enough to rough the defenders up a bit. I went up for a header with the centre half and, with both our eyes firmly fixed on the ball, we ended up heading each other. My head split open and I needed 20 odd stitches in a wound across my forehead where there is still a scar. I was so groggy that the youth coach, a former Burnley striker and future manager called Frank Casper, wanted to put me out of harm's way while the injury healed. He suggested playing right back because I could always stick my foot in and tackle. I did that for a couple of games and then came the time when I wanted to go back up front. Frank wouldn't have it. "No," he said. "I think you can be a better right back."

I was distraught. I liked the glory of scoring goals. Being a defender was alien to me. I tried to fight Frank and demanded to see the manager. But they held firm and a few weeks later I had a great game playing right back in the FA Youth Cup against Liverpool. The local paper gave me a good write-up and I thought: "I could get to like that." By accident, I had found a new position that was going to take me to the top level in English football. Who knows, if I had won the battle to stay up front and try to become the new Malcolm Macdonald, I might never have had a professional career.

Another regular job for the apprentices is to clean the boots of certain senior pros after training. I copped for

Steve Kindon, Brian Flynn and Leighton James. Now Brian was a real gentleman – but the other two were totally the opposite! They made my life hell – hammered me, absolutely murdered me. "Taffy" James, a Welsh international winger, had only just returned to Burnley in a then club record £165,000 move from Queens Park Rangers. He was a great footballer who went on to play 54 times for his country – but he was also an arrogant git. I had to call him "sir" and knock on the dressing room door to see if I could take his boots to be cleaned. It was the same with Kindon. He was about six foot three and just as wide. I would polish their boots until I could almost see my face in them.

Kindon would always warn me never to get boot polish on his laces. One morning he bawled out: "Lawsy, what's this?" He had some boot polish on his fingers, grabbed me in a headlock and rubbed it all over my face. Then he banged me into the dressing room wall. Life as an apprentice was tough but at least it taught you discipline and teamwork – even though we would often try to set each other up to get into trouble with the seniors.

It's very different for the trainees of today. When they join a club most of them think they have already got it made. But only a small percentage will be kept on. Rightly, there is more emphasis on coaching and also on education with trainees expected to spend time each week on studies. They are not asked to do as much donkey work around the ground. On the negative side, though, this has changed the discipline of young players and the way they talk to you. In my day you always had to be polite and never answer back. Compare that with an experience I had as manager of Scunthorpe when I overheard one of my pros ask a young trainee to clean his boots. The response? "Sorry, I can't, I'm just off for my massage!" Can you imagine how Kindon or James would have reacted to that!

I've now seen both sides of youngsters being told they haven't made the grade and are not being retained. It's the hardest job in the world for a manager. In my time at Burnley, Brian Miller had us in his office one by one. The three lads immediately in front of me each came out with tears in their eyes having been told their fate. I thought I would be next because nobody had given me any indication I would be one of the lucky ones. My heart was pounding and my hands were soaked in sweat. I was so worked up that I was also shaking when I entered the manager's office. He sat me down and I just stared at an object on his desk, a pencil, waiting for the news I dreaded. Miller was glancing at some paperwork and then began to talk. "You have seen some of the boys leave my office today disappointed," he said. "But I am NOT going to disappoint you. I am going to offer you a professional contract."

I was stunned and speechless. When I finally stood up to leave, I wanted to shout and skip and scream. But I knew there were boys out there in tears. Proud as I was for myself and my family, my thoughts were for the other lads at that time. They were my friends and we had gone through so much in two years together. I didn't want to rub their noses in it. Only two of us had been kept on, myself and Dean Walker, who was also from Newcastle. It was only later, when I rang my family, that I could let rip with my emotions – and I burst into tears.

My first season as a professional saw Burnley relegated to the Third Division, but it became a high spot for me personally. Despite a run of seven games without defeat, we were already down with Fulham and Charlton when we travelled to Watford for the final game of the 1979-80 season. I was included in the squad for the first time. It did not come as a big surprise because a lot of younger players had been in previous squads just for the experience of being part of things. I assumed it was my turn just to taste travelling with the team and learning from them.

At Vicarage Road I helped unload the kit from the bus and lay it out in the dressing room where, to my great shock, my name was on the teamsheet. I had been picked to play at right back instead of Ian Wood who had joined the club the previous summer after 500 games with Oldham. Discovering this only an hour or so before kick-off gave me little time to get nervous, but the tension boiled inside me as three o'clock approached. It was my first experience of playing in front of a proper-sized crowd. This was the day I had dreamed of since those distant times with Battle Hill in the Newcastle Junior League. But we lost 4-0 to Watford and, to make matters worse, their number 11 Keith Pritchett, my opposite number, scored twice. He only managed nine goals in his entire 133-game career with the Hornets and two of them were against me!

I thought I had a nightmare, my worst game ever. I felt nervous, didn't know what to do and when I came off I thought that was me finished where the first team was concerned; my career over before it had even started. If it was sink or swim, I had drowned.

Came the summer break back home and the first time I had felt depressed about football. The man who helped pick me up was Stewart Barraclough, who had played for Newcastle. Stewart, who knew my uncle, had a landscaping business and he invited me to go and work for him that summer to take my mind off things. It was all labouring, putting up fences, laying driveways and generally getting my fingers dirty. More than making me forget what happened at Watford, I found some muscles that summer. And when I went back to Turf Moor for pre-season training, I felt good, really strong. I got my opportunity again when Woodsy had a stinker and the manager threw me back in. This time I never looked back and played nearly every game that season as we finished eighth without ever getting into contention for promotion. The following season, 1981-82, proved to be memorable with Burnley finishing Third Division champions above Carlisle and Fulham who were also promoted. It was my first taste of success and I loved it. Not all of it, though. After clinching promotion with a 4-1 win at Southend we nearly drank our hotel dry. I had so much red wine it put me off the stuff for years!

The chairman was Bob Lord – and what a scary man he was. He ruled Burnley football club with a rod of iron and did the same at the FA. Everyone was wary of him, a massive man with big ears. When you walked down the corridor you had a job getting past him – and those ears of his. He never spoke to me, apart from the day I made my home debut. The corridors at Turf Moor were so narrow that two people could not pass without facing each other. I saw Bob Lord coming towards me and thought: "Oh shit. Do I pull off into another room and hide or do I just keep walking?" In the end, I just kept walking and we both had to stop so he could get his big belly round me. I was trying not to make eye contact in case I found myself in trouble. We had almost got past each other when he grabbed my arm and said: "Well done today." That was it and he walked on past.

I was lucky. We had a good team at Turf Moor in those days with players like former England man Martin Dobson, future international Trevor Steven, the Republic of Ireland's Mickey Phelan and Northern Ireland striker Billy Hamilton. I had massive respect for Dobson as a great old pro and he took me under his wing a bit. I'll always remember the advice he gave me. The social temptations for a young footballer are massive, even more so today. Martin would tell me: "Always look after number one. Keep focused on what you are aiming to be and don't let other people distract you. Then you can do very well."

It was my great fortune to be in a dressing room with a player like Martin, who was just the kind a manager needs to back him up when he is not there. The dressing room is the players' domain. It's where they can talk, express their feelings and let off steam at times. That is what players do and now, as a manager, I have respect for that. That is why it is important to have someone like Martin who the others can look up to and respect. Mind you, all that help he gave me came at a cost. He said one day: "Lawsy, is it right that you are something of a handyman as a builder? Well, you owe me. I have some work that I need doing in the garden." I thought it was only going to be a five-minute job. But I had to build a wall and dig out trenches. And he let me do it all by myself! So, yes, I do think I paid him back.

As a young player I would often get asked to go for a drink. Remembering Martin's advice, I would say "no." Probably some of the others thought I was a bit of a miserable bugger. Yet all I was bothered about was being a professional footballer and I wasn't going to let anything else get in the way. Nowadays, with all the money in the game, I see good young players and think that with two or three years of real hard graft and application there is a chance for them to be a millionaire. I always ask them the sort of question instilled into me by Martin Dobson: "Could you have given more? Could you have done better? Could you have been more professional?" If the answer is yes to any of those questions then they have not given it their best shot. They have let themselves down and that is why they have failed.

Brian Miller, the manager who gave me my first chance, was also a hard taskmaster. He was Burnley through and through, the only club he ever played for as a tough-tackling wing-half who was capped by England in 1961, the season after he helped the Clarets win the title. He was a big, sergeant major figure with closely-cropped ginger hair. Miller could be a bit loopy at times but we all had a lot of respect for him. He always said what he thought and wanted us to give our all for the club. You knew when he was not happy because his head would go completely red. That was a time to stay out of his way. At half-time in one game he was having a go at our centre half for not heading the ball. "I'm trying, boss," the lad protested. "Well, you're not trying hard enough," fumed Miller. "It's easy, I'll show you. Just imagine the ball is there." And he headed the door with such force that he left a massive hole in it. We all held our breath and went quiet. "Hey, look – it doesn't hurt, does it?" said Miller. But then he walked out of the room and I reckon he must have had some real pain.

I loved it at Burnley and had a real good rapport with the fans who voted me player of the season when we went up.

They were fanatical. Although they caned you for playing badly, the euphoria they whipped up in the good times was unbelievable. On the downside, Burnley were always a selling club. They always had to let their best players go. And the season after promotion we went straight back down again despite doing well in both cups. We got to the quarter-finals of the FA Cup and the semis in the League Cup with the club banking about £600,000. Unbeknown to me, this was to be my last season at Turf Moor. Brian Miller was sacked after our relegation in May 1983 and John Bond replaced him. His arrival was the beginning of the end for me.

We all knew about Bond's flamboyant past at Manchester City and sure enough he swaggered into Turf Moor, big cigar, big ego and plenty of jewellery. He was big and brash, and he seemed to have little respect for anyone in the dressing room. We went to the Isle of Man as part of our pre-season preparations and he was most bothered about stocking up with his cigars. Once, on the way to training, he stopped the bus to go into a tobacconists to get his beloved cigars.

All Bond was interested in was big, big, big. He brought in all his own cronies on big wages and didn't want anything to do with those who were already there. It was his big spending that was to be the demise of the club. Bond showed total disrespect for Martin Dobson. That hurt Martin – and it hurt me. Bond had never seen me play and he never spoke to me. The only time he did he had a real smug smile on his face and sneered: "You're not good enough. You're not wanted here." I was stunned. I'd hardly missed a game for four seasons. It was all so sad. I did not want to leave Burnley having been so happy there. But after Bond's arrival, I could not wait to get out and just took the first opportunity that came along. I was 21 years of age and had made 152 league appearances for the Clarets, scoring 12 goals.

But I had many cherished memories, once taking over in goal during a big derby against Blackpool. We were reduced to ten men when Alan Stevenson was sent off for kicking someone up the backside after a challenge he didn't like. For some reason I'd always fancied myself as a keeper and was first to volunteer to pick up the gloves. There I was, all five foot nine inches of me, trying to fill the goal against a Blackpool side which had Alan Ball pulling the strings. I'm sure Bally must have fancied his chances, but luckily I managed to pull off a couple of good saves – and we beat them! I got a lot of mickey-taking from the lads but was praised in the papers – maybe I missed my real vocation!

On the other side of the coin, I have always been blessed with a powerful shot. Once with the Clarets, I let fly from 25 yards with an effort that I swear was flying into the top corner until it hit the referee on the head and knocked him out cold. I don't remember what they called him, but I do know he had the name "Mitre" printed on his forehead! It was one of the funniest things I have ever seen, he keeled over completely.

Another time at Burnley I was "fortunate" enough to get an award for the best televised goal of the season. If only there had been Sky cameras present in those days, you would still be seeing it over and over again. Unfortunately, it was an own goal – from all of 45 yards. We were at Gillingham. Steve Bruce, who had the same Wallsend Boys Club connections as me, was playing for them – and he didn't half take the piss out of me afterwards. There was a ball coming across the field towards me from one direction and a player coming to put me under pressure from another. I thought I would just play it back to Alan Stevenson who was standing on the edge of his box. Somehow I hit it so sweetly that Alan was left vainly trying to grasp the ball out of the air as it flew over him and, without bouncing, hit the back of the net. Everybody in the ground burst out laughing – apart from me. I just wanted the ground to swallow me up. What quality, it got goal of the season on Gillingham's local TV. I've hit some good ones at the right end over the years – but none better than that!

It was at Burnley that I met and married my first wife Margaret – and where our daughter Danielle was born. Danielle became the "little miss" who arrived after my "big miss" of the night before! We were playing away at Crystal Palace in the fifth round of the FA Cup. With a quarter final place at stake, it was a big match for both clubs and a tight one as well. Defences were very much on top. Then we got a penalty and that was my job. It's a role I always used to relish and I had a good record. But this time I missed and the game finished goalless. Anyway, the drama of it all must have sent Margaret into labour and the very next day Danielle was born, prompting the newspaper headline: "Big Miss becomes a Little Miss." It was a happy moment for us and I was even happier when Burnley won the replay at Turf Moor before falling to Sheffield Wednesday at the next hurdle.

But my Burnley chapter would not be complete without mentioning Dora Whitefield, the dear old landlady who took me in after my unhappy experiences living in digs. I was the last of about six Burnley players, including Brian Flynn, who stayed with her over the years. Dora worked at the club and everybody loved her. She had lost her husband many years earlier and, with no family, lived on her own in a terraced house near the ground. Dora would stand no nonsense, mind you. She would bollock me good and proper if I did something wrong and would be there waiting, tapping her feet if I was back late. And she would threaten to tell the manager. But she taught me a lot and I loved her to bits.

I kept in touch with Dora through my various moves and I would sometimes visit her at weekends, by which time she was too old to take in players. She was on her own and yet I felt she was part of my family. I would fetch her across for weekends at my home occasionally as her health began to deteriorate. One night I got a phone call from the hospital in Burnley telling me Dora had fallen over wandering the streets. They said the only person she could turn to was me. Immediately I drove over to the hospital and said I would keep an eye on her as best I could. When she returned home I kept in touch with a neighbour to make sure she was okay. But it quickly became clear that, although her body was sound enough, her mind was going. Her doctors carried out tests which showed it was no longer safe for her to live on her own. Dora had to go into an old people's home, which was really hard for me as well because I had to take her out of the house where she had lived most of her life.

With no-one else around, I had to be the executor for Dora's estate and looked for a home for her. I didn't have a clue, really, but knew that the cost of the home would have to be offset by the sale of her house. How sad is that considering how hard she had worked all her life – and her husband, too, when he was alive, delivering milk around the streets of Burnley by horse and cart? Eventually we found a suitable home for Dora and her house was sold for little more than peanuts – £12,000, I think, was the price.

Dora would keep telling me she did not like her new place and wanted to go back to her own home. She seemed so upset, it made me wonder about the care she was getting. I was always supposed to arrange visits in advance, but one day I decided to turn up unannounced. And what I found turned my stomach. Dora was sitting there in a soaking wet armchair. Her clothes were sodden and she had obviously urinated. Worse, she had evidently been left like that for a while. No-one had gone to clean her up.

I knew immediately that this was not the right place for her. After all she had done in her life and all her help to others, she deserved better than that. I couldn't find anywhere in the Burnley district. By this time I was playing for Forest and a thought struck me: "Why don't I bring her over to the Nottingham area and find a home there so she can be near me?" I found somewhere suitable in the village where I lived. Dora still recognised me and I would try to see her every other day. Sadly, she had a fall and had to be transferred to hospital. By now her mind had completely gone, but one day she made me laugh when she suddenly blurted: "Brian, you know I can't give you children any more. I want you to go and find somebody else." I did my best to pacify her, saying it didn't matter and that I only wanted to be with her. But she was insistent and began shouting. Everyone in the room looked over at us and I am sure they must have wondered just what was going on!

Eventually Dora was well enough to return home where she passed away a few months later. My family were the only ones at the funeral. We arranged her final wish, which was to have her ashes spread near her husband's grave in Burnley. To me, Dora was much, much more than an old landlady. I just hoped that what I had been able to do for her made her final years as pleasant as possible. What made losing Dora doubly painful was that it came not long after I had seen my own mother die.

3

Between a Rioch and a Hard Place!

Misadventure – that would be my verdict on leaving Burnley in the summer of 1983 for what proved to be a short stay with Huddersfield Town. Not that I was sorry to see the back of John Bond. It's just that I ended up selling myself short with that transfer. Bond had been at West Ham in his playing career as a left back. Little did I know that I could have been swapping the claret and blue of Burnley for the claret and blue of the Hammers!

I signed for Huddersfield on August 26th, just 24 hours before the start of the 1983-84 season. They were newly promoted to Division Two under Mick Buxton who had been in charge for five years and had dragged the club all the way up from the basement. Mick needed a right back after selling Malcolm Brown to Newcastle for £250,000 and he convinced me it was the right move for my career. I had just signed a two-year contract when I got a call from Frank Casper, my mentor in my junior days at Turf Moor. He asked me why I had signed for Huddersfield and gave me a right rollocking. Then Frank mentioned that towards the end of my time at Burnley, West Ham had made an offer of around £170,000 for me. My fee in joining Huddersfield was just £50,000.

What a terrible stroke of business for both club and player! It was the sort of balls-up that could never happen today – agents would make sure of that. They weren't around in those days, of course. Burnley had turned down West Ham's bid. I was astonished, having known nothing about it. Clubs and managers dictated everything. That telephone call from Frank made me feel brilliant, didn't it? Not! Maybe in hindsight, if I had hung around at Burnley and put my name around, who knows?

But I'd been desperate to get away from Bond and had already committed myself to Huddersfield. They were at the old Leeds Road ground and, to be honest, it was falling to bits. I found life difficult there. At Burnley we were pampered. All the best kit was neatly laid out for us and we were made to feel like a million dollars. At Huddersfield they had an old lady called Nellie who washed all the kit – and it was over-washed to a degree where it would shrink. Here's something you won't believe, either. When I first put on some training kit, it was an old rugby top. Stitched on to the end of the sleeves were two old socks with the ends cut out. The idea was that if you got cold in training, you could warm your hands in the old socks instead of wearing gloves. When I put the top on, I could not see my hands for these socks. I thought: "My God, what have I done?" Just little things like that can leave a big impression on a player when he first joins a club. There were even times at Huddersfield when I had to wash my own gear, which was something we never had to do at Burnley.

Laundry lady Nellie had a habit of walking into the dressing room at Leeds Road. And she would do this when you had nothing on, standing stark naked! It was her way of belittling you. She certainly belittled me – no pun intended! The first time this happened she walked right up to me and I was so embarrassed. I didn't know where to look. And all the other lads were laughing! Nellie just said: "It's cold outside, isn't it!" Everyone was in stitches – apart from me. That was my welcome to Huddersfield. But all the lads loved Nellie and I got to love her, too. It was just her way of saying to new players that, wherever they had come from, they were back down to earth in West Yorkshire.

Nellie wasn't the only interesting character at Leeds Road. Leading the back line was a monster centre half called Sam Allardyce. He had a big heart and big authority. Sam couldn't run but he was a great organiser and worked the back four as a unit. He would dictate the offside trap, for instance. And it worked well – signs of the expert organiser and tactician he would become as an excellent manager, particularly at Bolton Wanderers. Also at Huddersfield was Mark Lillis – nicknamed "Buna" – who was later to become my assistant manager at Scunthorpe. Mark was a striker who worked his socks off and scored lots of goals. Later, he earned himself a big money move to Manchester City.

So it wasn't all bad in my 18 months at Huddersfield. I played nearly every game as we finished a comfortable mid-table in the club's first season back in the second tier. There was certainly a good team spirit – one thing that really stood out for me. Another was the number of hills there are in West Yorkshire. To be more accurate, some of them were like small mountains. And they were the favourite place for the manager to take us training. You could not run up them, you were bent over trying to get to the top, pushing your hands down on your thighs to keep moving up. They used to run us up and down those hills – and it was the first time I'd ever been physically sick in pre-season. Mind you, in all my time in the game I've yet to see a hill on a football pitch! And I shudder to think what Cloughie would have made of it . . .

Not that the geography was to blame for the first serious injury of my career, picked up in my second season at Huddersfield. I needed a cartilage operation which sidelined me for eight weeks. I'd never been able to settle and being out brought things to a head. I asked Mick Buxton for a move, telling him I wanted to get back closer to my North East roots. Being from that area himself, Mick did not stand in my way and said he did not want to keep a player who was unhappy. Then Middlesbrough came in with a £30,000 bid and off I went to Ayresome Park.

Willie Maddren and Bruce Rioch – you could not get a greater contrast than the two bosses I played under at Boro. Willie, the manager who signed me, was a bit like Brian Miller at Burnley in that he was a one-club man, having played nearly 300 Middlesbrough games during a nine-year period in which he won England Under 23 caps as a defender. Then, after staying on at Ayresome, Willie followed Jack Charlton, John Neal, Bobby Murdoch and Malcolm Allison into the managerial hot-seat. I've never met a nicer guy than Willie. He was perhaps too nice to be a manager and one or two players abused his good nature. If I have one criticism to make of him, it's that he did not crack down hard enough on those players. He trusted them too much and they let him down.

At that time, Middlesbrough were on a downturn that was to bring the club to its knees. After eight seasons in the top flight, financial problems were kicking in when I joined them in March, 1985. They were in the Second Division and in disarray. Yet Boro were closer to my home in Newcastle, the factor which convinced me it was the right move. And, for all the problems off the field, I really enjoyed my time there. For starters, I took to the supporters and they took to me. What cemented the relationship was the survival drama at the end of that season as we avoided relegation by the skin of our teeth. We had to win the final game at Shrewsbury – and I scored with a 25-yard screamer in a 2-0 victory. You would have thought we'd won the cup! Our fans ran on to the pitch and carried us off. It was all a bit embarrassing really.

We all thought that this was a turning point, that things would get better. Instead, they got worse. We opened the next season with just one win in the first nine matches and Boro reacted by bringing in Bruce Rioch as coach. Rioch, a Scottish international midfielder renowned as a hard man, had just had his first taste of management at Torquay. A spot of bother led to him resigning. We found out in our first training session under Bruce that his reputation was for real. This was on a Friday when it is usually nice and easy.

But Bruce came in and boomed: "I want shin pads on and I want you to go like hell into tackles. If it's 50-50 I want you to go in as though your life depends on it. And I don't care who it's against."

So, instead of the normal thing of rehearsing set plays and brushing up on the opposition, he had us fighting with each other. And by hell, that's what he got. There were one or two fall-outs and I think that's exactly what Bruce wanted. We had a young winger called Peter Beagrie. He and I went in for a challenge – but then both of us pulled out because it was the day before a match and we could have hurt each other. Bruce stopped the session there and then. He ranted and raved at us. And he threatened to drop us there and then.

When the session restarted, Bruce joined in. Just a minute or two later I found myself confronted by him as he ran with the ball at his feet. There was no doubt in my mind what had to be done, no pulling out this time. I was mad, he had just had a right go at me and I had to let him know I'd learned my lesson. So I flew in and really whacked him, knocking him on his backside. I took the ball and everything else. You could cut the tension as the game stopped and all the other players looked at me, no doubt thinking "you stupid git." But Bruce said nothing. He just stood up, brushed himself down and insisted on carrying on.

The session seemed endless – probably for a reason you're about to discover – and we'd been playing flat out for another 45 minutes or so when Bruce found the opportunity to get me back. I remember both of us going for the ball as it bounced off the floor and then he gave me a forearm smash that nearly knocked my teeth out. I'd expected something like that and knew I would have to take it. And almost immediately, he then blew time! Whether Bruce had a sneaking admiration for me I never found out. But I could see the logic of what he was trying to do. He wanted to instil some fight in us as we battled to avoid the drop.

Unfortunately, it didn't work out. By coincidence the final Saturday of the season again took us to Gay Meadow to face the Shrewsbury side we'd beaten to survive 12 months earlier. This time there was no happy ending. Blackburn and Sunderland, the two teams we were trying to catch, both won at home while we went down 2-1. So Middlesbrough plunged into the third tier for only the second time in their history. There was the expected knee-jerk reaction from the board. Out went Willie Maddren as manager to be replaced by Rioch.

All season we had read reports about a cash crisis but none us realised how grave the situation had become – until that summer. I suppose we had tunnel vision – all that mattered to us was playing and getting paid. Naively, we felt everything else would take care of itself, as it always did. After all, clubs were always crying wolf about money. And they always seemed to survive somehow. It was only slowly that we began to grasp that Middlesbrough really were in dire straits.

The final realisation came during pre-season when one morning we turned up to find the gates shut and padlocked. There'd been no actual warning that this was about to happen and everyone was shocked. All we could do was sit around and wait. Eventually Bruce came and tried to explain the predicament. He said there were severe financial difficulties but asked us to be patient as he wanted to keep us all together.

But that patience was stretched to the limit when six weeks went by with nowhere proper to train – and no pay! This, by the way, was a world away from today's salaries – although even in 2012 salaries lower down the scale bear no relation to the amounts the top stars are getting. I wasn't on a lot, that's for sure. I had a wife and young family to support, a mortgage to pay and a bank manager asking me for money. Several others were in the same boat. Panic took hold and as a group we decided to consult the Professional Footballers Association, which wasn't an automatic reflex at the time. The PFA said that if the club were not paying us then we were entitled to a free transfer. In short, they told us we could just walk out. But we didn't want to do that. What we really wanted was to be paid. As club skipper, I had to take a lead and gained the support of Peter Beagrie and Archie Stephens.

We took the club to a tribunal which was held in Oldham. To get there I had to borrow a "car" – or more accurately, an old banger – from Bruce Rioch. My own sponsored club car had been taken away. It was a bright red Vauxhall Cavalier with the words Middlesbrough Football Club written right across the length of it in big white letters. As you can imagine, it stood out a mile. A club car was supposed to be a perk but this was more of a chain round my neck – because there were times when I couldn't go anywhere in it, particularly after we'd lost.

Anyway, with the car seized back by the club's administrators, the manager gave me this so-called vehicle to drive to Oldham. It was more like a skip on wheels. It spluttered all the way as I drove with Archie and Beags to the tribunal but we got there, just. The hearing ruled in our favour, saying we could quit Middlesbrough with immediate effect. In fact, the chairman of Oldham, who headed the commission, tried to poach me almost there and then!

As we left for home, the car broke down at the first roundabout. Beags and Archie had to get out and push it in the pouring rain for about a mile before I could get the engine going again. But at least we had some shelter from the storm breaking over Middlesbrough. Either they were going to pay us or we were on our way. The squad they had left were all kids, including a young Gary Pallister. I think I was the oldest at 23. Finally, the club found some money to pay us and Bruce came round to our houses with a cheque. Great credit to him for that.

Needless to say, it was the worst possible preparation for a new season. We trained on any piece of land we could find, mainly in local parks where we got changed in cars. And we still didn't know if Boro would stay in business. But we stuck together, that's the important thing. We only had a squad of about 14 left and yet that summer proved to be a huge turning point for Middlesbrough FC. A true saviour emerged to forge a vibrant, healthy club for the modern era.

First, though, we had to borrow a ground for our first "home" game of the 1986-87 season. The match, against Port Vale, was played at the Victoria Ground, the home of nearby Hartlepool. It was a sell-out as our fans rallied round to fill the tiny stadium. Still unable to bring in any new players, Bruce was short in midfield and asked me to switch there for him. I'd never played that role before, but these were desperate times. Archie Stephens struck a belter and we drew that opening game 2-2. Afterwards, we were emotionally drained. Somehow the troubles had bonded us together and the fans, too, could sense new hope.

A very young man was starting to appear in the boardroom and it turned out that he was funding a lot of expenses out of his own pocket. His name was Steve Gibson. What a tremendous guy! Soon afterwards, the gates were unlocked and we were back at Ayresome Park. We got on a roll and never looked back . . . unbeaten in our opening 10 games before losing 3-1 at home to Blackpool.

That didn't stop a promotion assault and formulated my belief that success is mostly down to team spirit and togetherness. That is something that has stayed with me and I am big on it as a manager. You can have 11 good individuals but if they don't bond as a group then you are never going to achieve anything.

For all that, I remained a reluctant midfield player, the position I played almost throughout that successful season. I kept going back to see Bruce and remind him what he'd said; that he was looking to bring in someone else so that I could go back to right-back. "But you're doing well," he would reply. "I'm not enjoying it, though," I would insist. Mind you, I scored 10 goals that season – and I'd be lying if I said I didn't enjoy that! And as the midfield anchorman, I had good energy and liked to get forward.

An unbeaten run in our last 13 games ensured Middlesbrough were promoted behind champions Bournemouth and so returned to the second tier. But I wasn't part of it. Back in January we'd played at home to Preston on a freezing afternoon in the third round of the FA Cup. In the second half I went up for a challenge, came down first and one of their players landed on top of me. It felt like a bullet had gone off in my knee. I managed to hobble on but after the game, which we lost 1-0, I was on the treatment table with my knee swollen. I thought it was cartilage trouble again and so did the physio. After a few days' treatment the swelling went down and Bruce Rioch assured me it WAS cartilage trouble. He said he'd had similar problems and that I'd be okay.

However, a couple of weeks later my knee just blew up. We were playing at home to Bristol Rovers when we were awarded a penalty five minutes before half-time. As the regular spot-kick taker, I put the ball down and had a picture in my mind of what I was going to do. As usual, I was just going to blast it into the bottom corner. I was so confident I would even show the goalkeeper which way I was going. Anyway, all I can remember is running up and then landing in a heap. As I bent my leg to kick the ball there was a huge explosion in my knee, like a shotgun crack. I collapsed but with the momentum I had, I still touched the ball and screwed it well wide. Can you imagine the embarrassment? I remember players calling me a "wanker" after what seemed to them, and everyone else in the ground, a dreadful miss. But then they realised I had a real problem. I was in agony, stretchered off in excruciating pain.

Just as painful is my belief, which has stretched from that day to this, that the real damage was done in that cup tie with Preston a few days earlier. If only I had known then! The dreadful realisation dawned as I came round following surgery in hospital. Far from having cartilage trouble, I had torn my cruciate ligament. That was almost a death knell for footballers in those days. I have never been more devastated in my life. There I was, still in my early twenties, and my whole career was suddenly in the balance.

Would I be able to play again? That was the question flashing through my mind as I lay in a hospital bed. But I couldn't bring myself to say it out loud. Finally, I plucked up the courage to ask the doctor – and he couldn't answer me. Tears came flooding out, I couldn't stop myself. I was sobbing like a child. The players were gutted for me as they came visiting. I was in plaster from hip to ankle and the pain was still killing me.

Bruce Rioch tried to raise my spirits. He said he had come back after several big operations and he brought a six-pack of lager, saying: "You're going to be in a bit of pain, get that lot down you." But that didn't stop me wondering what I was going to do if this was the end of my career. I still wanted to stay in football somehow. Worse, I hadn't heard of any other player coming back from a cruciate ligament injury. But the doctors told me about Scottish international George Burley who was then playing for Sunderland. They got me his number, so I rang George and had a real heart to heart with him. It proved to be the best two hours' conversation I've ever had with anybody. George was brilliant for me. He told of his similar injury and of the long road back before he returned to playing. If George could do it, so could I. That telephone call was the turning point. Doubt was replaced by determination, despair was drowned by hope. Brian Laws was not finished yet!

Middlesbrough sent me to the FA's recently established rehabilitation unit at Lilleshall where I worked from morning till night for 15 weeks. It was the longest any player had spent there. "You can lead a horse to water but you can't make it drink," was the philosophy of the specialists at Lilleshall. In other words, you can't be half-hearted and wait for some miracle cure. You have to do the hard work yourself. I was totally single-minded and went flat out. But after months of hard work, I still couldn't bend my knee more than 40 degrees. And it has to bend in order to stretch the ligament.

They told me they were going to have to physically force my knee back. I remember three people holding me down on the edge of the bed. One held my shoulders, another pressed down on my hip and the third pushed my leg. But my knee was just like a rod. It simply wouldn't bend and I was screaming from the pressure they were exerting. I was biting on a pillow with the blood rushing to my face. We tried and tried because this was the only way. Finally, they said I would have to go under anaesthetic to relax me because all my muscles had tensed up so much. I remember waking up feeling drowsy and wondering what the hell was happening because I found myself sitting on a bike! They wanted to get my knee going as quickly as possible – but I was to find out later that it had snapped again during all the efforts to bend it.

There was a lot of soul-searching to do. Could I go through all the hard slog at Lilleshall again, having already been out of football for months? I'm glad I went back because the medical team found a huge difference in the movement of my knee. The encouragement enabled me to throw myself back into the work and I built up the top half of my body, too. I was much, much stronger all round.

Former England defender Colin Todd had joined the coaching staff by the time I went back to Middlesbrough. Colin would take me every afternoon for ball work, just the two of us, on the Ayresome Park pitch. We did running, passing and shooting. But there was a psychological barrier to overcome and Colin knew it. The fear factor. I was a player who tackled hard, but every time I watched a game during my long absence it made me cringe to see players going in full tilt. I would think to myself that I would never be able to do that again. Colin and Bruce both knew I had to learn how to get physical again. And it was important that the other players had to get physical with me. I think they were scared of what they might do to me. And I was scared, too. Every time I had to tackle in training I was sweating.

So Colin coaxed me gently back into the art and psychology of it. First we would take one step back from each other and then both go for the ball. Then we would take two steps back – and so on. It was all very tentative. I remember once ducking out and lifting my foot. It made contact with Colin's shin and nearly ripped the skin off. He turned round and yelled: "You bastard!" And there were a number of other occasions when he called me every name under the sun before my confidence steadily grew and I was able to tackle properly again. I had a few reserve games and finally, after more than a year out, I returned to the first team squad as a substitute, oddly enough against previous side Huddersfield.

This was March 12, 1988, and they threw me on in the second half – on the right wing so I could stay out of trouble. But not out of the headlines – for the right reasons – as it turned out. Their keeper sliced a clearance which fell to me and I sent it straight back crashing into the back of the net from about 30 yards. It was fairytale stuff on my comeback and I felt a million dollars. The players were all over me – such a wonderful feeling. They knew how hard I'd worked to recover and it was all very emotional. We won 2-0 into the bargain, another vital result for a team that was heading towards a second successive promotion.

Rioch had been able to keep the squad together and we had players emerging with real quality. There were men like Gary Pallister, Tony Mowbray and Colin Cooper in addition to Stephens, Beagrie and goalscoring legend Bernie Slaven. It was a GOOD team and the spirit was FANTASTIC. No surprise that we found ourselves challenging for a place in the First Division. Ayresome Park was packed out as we took on Leicester City in the final game. Aston Villa were just a point behind in third place. They were away at Swindon and all we had to do was match Villa's result to return to the top flight after an absence of six years. It was only two years since the club nearly went to the wall but that seemed like light years ago.

The whole town was alive and this was going to be our day, party time. But the fates didn't follow the script. Come the second half we were losing 2-1. Then we got a message that Villa were also behind. So we still thought we were going up. It was only after the final whistle that we found to our horror that some wires had got crossed and Villa had actually drawn 0-0 at Swindon. It meant they had climbed above us into second place by the incredibly narrow margin of having scored four more goals over the course of the season. Both of us had 78 points and an identical goal difference of plus 27 – but Villa had scored 67 goals to our 63 and that was enough to nick them automatic promotion.

That left us to face Bradford City in the play-offs. Whether it would have made any difference had we been told the right score from the Villa match, we will never know. It was all a huge blow, but we managed to pick ourselves up for those play-off games. Although we lost the first leg 2-1 at Valley Parade, we were confident of overcoming the deficit at our place. This time, in front of another packed house, we did the business 2-0 to go through to face Chelsea – then battling to stay in the top division – in the final. In those days, the team that finished third bottom in the First Division had a chance to preserve their status through the play-offs. Another difference from today was that the final was also played over two legs.

We played brilliantly to beat the Londoners 2-0 at Ayresome. Nevertheless, we faced a tough and intimidating return leg at Stamford Bridge where Chelsea fans had a reputation for violence. Then something happened that put all these worries, hopes and fears into true perspective.

Just as I was about to board the team coach for the journey south I was pulled to one side to take a call from my family. The message was that my mother was desperately ill and I was needed at home. I had to pull out of the Chelsea game and rushed to join my father, brother and sister at Mum's bedside. Sadly, she passed away. Suddenly, all the buzz, excitement and anticipation of the Chelsea game was forgotten. It did not matter to me anymore. My priorities were with my family, making the arrangements for Mum's funeral. Just as she passed away, we had promised her that we would look after Dad. Her death perhaps hit John and Maureen even harder than me. Having followed a football career and lived away, I had lost some of the closeness that they enjoyed with her – and I envied them that. But it was a sacrifice I had to make and at least my earnings from football enabled me to buy Dad a little bungalow in Washington so that he could be just around the corner from Maureen. I think she needed that, too, because she had been real close to Mum, who had always been a strong character. Mum also had an unbelievable appetite for hard work. She would have three jobs on the go at the same time, working morning, noon and night to support the family budget. Mum was always working and I can never remember her taking even a day off while I was a young boy at home.

Happily for Middlesbrough, they won through the play-offs, losing just 1-0 in London to triumph 2-1 on aggregate. There were some violent scenes on the terraces but Boro were back in the top division and the town was alight. A short tour of Canada was arranged for players and staff to celebrate. Of course, I couldn't be part of that. I was still in a daze dealing with Mum's funeral. And matters were made worse when some official looking correspondence from the club dropped through the letterbox at home.

I was out of contract that summer but some haggling with Bruce Rioch towards the end of the season had resulted in agreement on a new two-year deal. I was a popular player on Teesside and when the manager announced the contract in the local press, the fans were happy. But the letter from the club contained a shock. The terms were totally different to the ones I had shaken hands on with Bruce.

I thought there must have been some mistake and immediately tried to get Bruce on the phone in Canada. When I finally got hold of him he said he wouldn't discuss it over the phone. He wanted me to go out to Canada. So the day after Mum's funeral I jetted across the Atlantic to join the rest of the squad. Finally, I was able to confront Rioch about the reduced contract and it was quickly evident to me that it was not the club who had made a mistake. I asked him why he had gone back on his word and reneged on the deal. He just said he had changed his mind! My response was immediate and to the point. I fumed: "(Fuck you, Bruce) – I will never play for you again."

Obviously he could not have picked a worse time for a fight with me, although there was still a point of principle at stake. I walked away, went back to my room in the hotel and let the whole emotion of what I had just been through come flooding out. I felt let down, I was angry and I cried. I wanted to come back home, but I had to stay with the squad in Canada and Bruce made me play in one of the games. I just "walked" through it, went through the motions, that's how disgusted I was.

Rioch was furious and after the game threatened me in a way I would not want to be treated by anybody. We had a stand-up barney in front of the other players. Frankly, I didn't care. I thought the way I had been treated was disgusting. Bruce told me I would never play for the club again and tried to send me home there and then. And I would have been more than happy to go.

There was nothing else for it but to leave Middlesbrough. But this was well before "Bosman" and there was no freedom of movement for out-of-contract players in those days. If you wanted to leave, your club had a right to claim a transfer fee.

While I was waiting to fly back from Canada with the rest of the squad, I rang home and asked my wife Margaret to send a letter to every club in the top two divisions informing them I was looking for a move. By the time I arrived back, a few clubs had already made enquiries on the phone with Crystal Palace manager Steve Coppell among them.

Then I got a call that was to provide the most exciting twist of my career. It was from Ronnie Fenton, the assistant manager at Nottingham Forest, and everyone knew who was in charge there. I just thought it was Beags playing one of his tricks again. He had caught me out like that before. But the phone rang again and the voice on the other end said: "This is Ronnie Fenton at Nottingham Forest, Brian Clough wants a word." I was still convinced it was a prank. I shouted "bollocks" and put the phone down again. Then it rang once more. Once again it was the voice that claimed to be Ronnie Fenton. But this time he put me straight through to someone else . . .

4

Young Man, Are You Good Enough to Play for Me?

Still I wondered if Beags had got me again. He was very good, you know. A few weeks earlier I'd had a call purporting to come from the Blackburn Rovers manager Don Mackay. It was Mackay, for sure, right down to the Scottish accent. Or so I thought. He said he'd made a £500,000 bid for me. Was I interested? Yes, I was. We talked for about 10 minutes. It was all so convincing that when a few days passed and I'd heard nothing more, I started to worry. It was only then that Beags owned up. He'd been hoping I'd make an even bigger fool of myself by putting in a follow-up call to the real Mackay at Blackburn.

But even Beags couldn't take off Cloughie. There was no doubting the voice on the other end of the phone. You couldn't imitate that unmistakable drawl. All right, some have but you know what I mean. I had goose bumps – it's him, it's really him! The great man himself – a title winner with both Derby County and Nottingham Forest for whom he had monumentally lifted two European Cups. And he was ringing me. I was speechless. And automatically I stood up next to the phone. That's how much respect I had for a man I had never met.

"Now young man, how would you like to play for Nottingham Forest?" It was like that "I do" moment for nervous couples getting married. Somehow I managed to find my voice in time to say: "I'd love to."

"Well then," said Cloughie. "Get yourself down here, I want to talk to you. And bring your wife, bring your children."

Quickly we made arrangements to travel down to Nottingham and Ronnie Fenton was there to greet us. He started by showing us round the City Ground – "I'd love a bit of this," I thought to myself. Eventually we went inside and Ronnie sat me down in an office next to his. Then in came Cloughie and again I immediately stood up. It was an instinctive reaction. He was simply the most famous face in football at that time. Cloughie was on every television station and every newspaper, you couldn't miss him. And every player in the land would have died for the opportunity of going to work with that man. Here I was with that very chance. There was no way I was going to turn down anything he offered.

To this day I remember how he looked. He was wearing what amounted to his uniform for work – blue tracksuit bottoms, white trainers and, of course, the famous green jersey. You'd never see him suited and booted. "Welcome to the club," said Cloughie. "But I just want to ask you something. Are you a good player or a bad player?"

I thought it was a strange question – but then this was Cloughie. "Well, I think I must be alright if you're looking at me," I replied. Not a bad response, eh? Actually, a bit too good.

"Ooh smart arse," said Cloughie. "There is a reason for me asking you that question – because I haven't seen you play!"

I came back with: "So why have you got me here?" Again, a wee bit too clever. "We've got a right smart arse here, haven't we?" Cloughie went on. "It's Ronnie Fenton who has seen you and he thinks you're worth a chance. ARE YOU?"

There was only one answer to that. "Yes."

"Well, I'm going to tell you something else," said the great man. "You're not getting in my side unless you PROVE you're good enough."

At this point I dared to ask about terms. Another mistake. "TERMS?" he bellowed. "You don't say anything to me, you get what you get given here, and that's it! When you play in my team, then you can talk terms. That's what we do here. Are you interested?"

In truth, I was so excited about the prospect of signing for Forest and playing in the First Division for this inspirational man that I would have accepted almost anything he offered me. Then Cloughie turned to his assistant and said: "Ron, how much is he going to cost me?" Fenton told him he had spoken to Middlesbrough and they were asking between £400,000 and £500,000.

"No way are we going to pay that," fumed the manager. Turning back to me, he said: "I will tell you now son, you can sign this contract but if we have to pay anything more than £100,000 you can forget it."

The clubs could not agree a compromise and so it went to a tribunal, leaving me to wet myself about the possible verdict. Could my dream be snatched away? Yes, we had all the evidence about what Boro had originally offered me and how much that had then been reduced. But I had to wait until the end of July for the tribunal to sit – which was after the start of pre-season training.

Meantime, Ronnie Fenton took me and my wife around Nottingham to look at housing. We had a brand new four-bedroomed place in Middlesbrough and I expected prices in Notttingham to be a little higher. Ronnie showed us round an estate in West Bridgford constructed by the same company that had built our house on Teesside. Great, I thought. Except that the asking price turned out to be £240,000. And bear in mind, this was back in the summer of 1988. "I can't afford that on the peanuts I'm getting at Forest," I told Ronnie. He suggested I'd better have another word with Cloughie. So back I went to the City Ground to explain to the manager that prices in the area were much higher than I expected when I agreed terms.

"Not my problem," boomed Cloughie. But after a moment or two he came up with a solution. "I'll tell you what, I'll do you a deal. I have a house that you can use. It's a club house that Stuart Pearce will be moving out of shortly. Here are the keys. When he has gone, you can move in. In the meantime, you can live in a hotel. Okay? Right, now piss off!" I went away wondering just how I was going to be able to afford to live in Nottingham. "I'd better get in the first team – and quickly," I thought.

But first there was that tribunal. It was held at the Highfield Road ground of Coventry City. For the first time since our row I had to meet up again with Bruce Rioch – and in a very small room. He tried to be as polite as possible but showed some embarrassment. I was feeling uncomfortable, too. I didn't want to be there with that man – I still didn't understand why he had treated me the way he did. Somehow I overcame the urge to have a go at him. But more than anything else, I was scared. What if the tribunal set too high a fee? Then I'd have to go back to Boro and Rioch. I remembered Cloughie's words. He wasn't prepared to pay more than £100,000 and Boro were asking for nearly half-a-million.

At least I had the chance to spell out in detail everything that had happened to me at Ayresome Park, what had been offered and how the club and manager had gone back on their word. I could sense that the panel were not happy with the way I had been treated. But would they set a low enough figure? That was the doubt gnawing away at me as I left the room and Rioch went in to say his piece. Ronnie Fenton was with me when we were all called back in for some closing questions before the panel retired to consider their verdict. It was nip and tuck.

The wait seemed forever even though it was slightly under a couple of hours. Then came the announcement. The transfer fee was fixed at £125,000. My heart sank. I was gutted. That was £25,000 too much. I felt like the condemned man as Ronnie rang the City Ground to tell Cloughie the news. There was a pause as Ronnie awaited his instructions from the other end of the phone. Then he turned to me and smiled. Cloughie WAS prepared after all to pay the extra.

What a relief – a huge relief. It was not until much later in life that I began perhaps to understand just a little where Bruce Rioch was coming from with his decision over me. I had just come back from a major injury and maybe he thought I was not good enough for Middlesbrough who were themselves newly promoted to the top flight. Possibly he wanted to use the money he could get for me to strengthen another area of his squad. I don't bear any grudges. Not now. But it was the way he went about it that

I have never been able to accept. I admire Bruce for what he has achieved in the game. He is a very good coach. But he is also a strict disciplinarian. Maybe that was his trouble when he got the manager's job at Arsenal. The big boys don't like those methods and Bruce couldn't change.

Pre-season training at Forest was another eye-opener. I turned up to be surrounded by famous faces. There were internationals like Stuart Pearce and Des Walker. "Oh, my God," I thought. I was just in awe of everybody. But while on the team coach on the way to training at Wollaton Park I made up my mind that I was going to impress my new team-mates.

Off we went at the start of a run. I was a good runner, I didn't mind that. But then for some reason the whole group started walking. Then we jogged and then we walked! What's going on here? I'm at the front, thinking: "Come on, let me off, just let me show how I can run. Come on somebody, go."

Eventually Pearcey moved up next to me and said: "Who the fuck are you? What do you think you're doing? Hang fire, get back here and just watch what the rest of us do." We dawdled round to the end of the training course and I had hardly broken sweat. Then Pearcey hammered me again. "That's the hardest session we've had because of all your pushing at the front," he stormed. I just said: "Well, if that's hard then bloody hell!" Pearcey just insisted: "Take it easy, you'll learn." I felt certain things would get harder, but they didn't. In fact, it was the easiest pre-season I'd ever known.

I had to do more, I needed it. So I did the work on my own, running the streets because I wasn't used to Forest's type of training, it wasn't my way. I also went out and bought myself a mountain bike. I would ride from home to the training ground and back. This was to satisfy me, no-one else. But the feeling soon wore off. What I was to realise was that the one thing Forest had was quality players. Their motto was: The ball runs quicker than any player. We keep it – let the opposition chase it. So to play for Forest you didn't have to be super fit, you just had to be decent on the ball. Training was built around five-a-side. It was light, it was enjoyable and it finished quickly. Cloughie used to come down and watch us but he never joined in. I have never experienced coaching like it – because there was none. You'd just have Liam O'Kane and Archie Gemmill supervising us down at the training ground. I kept waiting for Brian Clough to emerge as this tactical genius, master-tactician, set-play merchant and all that type of stuff. It had to come sometime, I thought. But let me tell you, I was there for over six years and never saw a thing.

But what Cloughie had was this aura about him. People said he was intimidating but he wasn't really, or at least not in a bad way. Yes, you had to watch what you said. He'd make you feel comfortable and yet uncomfortable at the same time. It's hard to describe. But there's no doubt that he brought out the best in people. And he was to give me the best years of my career.

5

Learning the Hard Way – and Not Hitting Desmond Walker Hard Enough!

This was the start of six-and-a-half fabulous years at the City Ground, helping Nottingham Forest to five Wembley finals and grabbing myself a B international cap for England. But even after all of that I still have a confession to make to Cloughie. He asked me if I was a good player. I lied! If I'm honest – and this is as good a time and place to be candid as any – I wasn't a good player at all. I was only an average one. That's the way I still class myself despite all that we achieved as a team. But that was the trick; we were a great unit and I fitted into Cloughie's vision of how it should be put together. Beyond that, he brought the best out of all of us. But you also have to remember that I came in on the back of a few bad buys, signings like Justin Fashanu and Ian Wallace. This was after Cloughie's split from Peter Taylor, who'd always identified the players, and maybe he was questioning his judgment. As for me, joining him at Forest would either make me or break me.

At first, as I've mentioned, I couldn't see how it all worked. There was the low-key training and the nonexistent coaching. Bear in mind that I'd always been used to sergeant-major type managers who regimented you. Stand still, move there. Suddenly I was in an environment where I had to think for myself. But there was coaching of a sort and it would be dramatic – like being taken off during a game to teach you a lesson.

Another culture shock was the atmosphere in the dressing room before a game. I'd always been used to having a lot of sound around me and I was one of the really noisy ones. It was the clenched fist approach amid cries of "come on boys, let's get out there and get 'em." At Forest, as I was quickly to learn, things were very different and at first I found it difficult to know how to act. Cloughie would only come in about 10 to 15 minutes before kick-off. That was about the only time you would really see him and, of course, he'd be wearing that old green jersey of his. Or one of them. I can only assume he must have had a dozen. He would wear one all the time, so surely it can't have been the same jersey every time.

Another part of the dressing room ritual would be that he would sit down and every player would also be sitting down. In most dressing rooms there's random movement, some sitting, some standing, some kicking a ball against the wall. At Forest no-one would be walking around. We'd all be sitting down on the benches and Cloughie would say: "Relax, get your feet out, lean back and cross your arms – and just think!" He would also put a towel down in the middle of the floor and place a football on it. Then he would say: "That's what you play with. None of this bullshit in the air, you're playing with the ball. I want you to caress that football as though it's your wife or your girlfriend – and in some cases like it's your boyfriend! You treat that football with respect and it will treat you back with that same respect. I want you to be gentle with it, pass it, love it and it will give you those things back. And when you are 1-0 up, do you know what you do? You BOOT that bloody ball in the stand, row Z. And they can't score from there. That's how you win a game."

Rightly, Cloughie earned praise for keeping it simple and you can't have it put any more simply than that. Where so many others over-complicate the game, there was no mystique to his mastery of it. And there can't have been any deeper secrets to his approach because our dressing room door was always left wide open. This was something else that was different from all my previous clubs. We could often hear music blasting down the corridor from where our opponents were getting changed. And then the sound of their boot studs as they left the dressing room, followed by some loud voices as they geed themselves up for the start of the game. They would pass by our open door and look in to see us sat back, all relaxed with legs stretched out. How intimidating was that! But here was Cloughie at work, the master of psychology.

There were never any last-minute coaching instructions. Cloughie would send the coaches out if they tried to say anything. "You've had all week to do that," he would remind them. It was all part of Cloughie's mind games to let the opposition see us like that. And he would use the pitch as his training ground. If he saw you doing something wrong on the field he would take action there and then, not wait until some session in the middle of the following week. I discovered this to my cost when we were playing Manchester United in front of a full house at the City Ground. It was the most embarrassing thing that has happened to me in my life.

About twenty five minutes into the game I found myself running down the right hand side of the pitch into United's half. A massive gap opened up and I could see Nigel Clough, the son of the manager, asking for the ball at his feet. Then I heard Neil Webb on the other side of the park shouting my name and also demanding the ball. So instead of playing a pass in to Nigel, I played a blind ball in the direction of Webb on the other side. And, you've guessed it, the pass got cut out. Worse, much worse, away went Manchester United who got past Stuart Pearce for the first time and in came a cross to the far past. I'd got back in time to go for it – and so did Mark Hughes. Bang, on the volley, Sparky cracked it into the top corner of the net. Great goal, even I had to admit that. But something inside told me that I was really in deep mire. I turned round and waited for us to kick off. Instead Cloughie kicked off. Before we re-started, the number 2 card came up and I was dragged off.

It was a total shock. I'd been playing well up to that point but Cloughie had a bee in his bonnet about this one mistake. Frankly, I was disgusted and I was also determined not to go to the halfway line and shake hands with my replacement. Instead, I gave Cloughie probably the dirtiest look I've ever given anyone. I was not a happy bunny. Back in the dressing room, I had a bath and got changed. I was waiting for them at half-time as the team came into the dressing room, still losing 1-0. Cloughie came in and just sat down. Everyone else sat down, too . . . just waiting. Because everyone knew what was going to happen – except me.

Finally Cloughie stood up and strode slowly over

towards me. "If you ever look at me like that again I'm going to knock your head off," he growled. "Do you know why I brought you off, you idiot?" I told him I guessed it was because I had not passed the ball to Nigel and had given away possession. "Well done you IDIOT," he ranted on. "That is why I brought you off. Don't you ever do that again – and you're playing next Saturday, so get out of my sight!" That was his way. Dropping you down and bringing you up. There was certainly method in that madness and, for me, an unforgettable lesson learned – with the chance of putting it right in the next game.

Even so, I was still seething when I went into the players lounge during the second half. My wife was there with the kids. Normally I was near enough the last in but this time I was the first. "You're early!" she said. It turned out she had no idea I had been subbed. Now that tells you what some women are like, especially at football clubs. Not all women. Just the ones who appear to have no interest in the game, apart from yapping! I just went mad.

Here's another example of learning on the job from earlier in my time at Forest. It was during my first pre-season trip with them, a tour of Sweden. What you find about the Swedish club teams is that they are great for 20 minutes, then they fade and you end up scoring five or six goals in the later stages. Although I had been playing midfield at Middlesbrough, full-back was my position and Cloughie put me in at right back for one of the games, playing behind Franz Carr. Now Franz was as quick as anything, like lightning in fact. But he was more of an individual, capable of brilliant runs and crosses. I remember playing a ball in to Franz and then running past him, looking for a return pass so that I could get in a cross.

That was the theory! In practice, Franz lost the ball and this Swedish team went straight up the other end to score. Cloughie caned me for it. "This is where you learn your trade and know your team-mates," he said. "See that idiot there (pointing at Franz). Support him, yes. But never run past him because he will never give you the ball and it will make you look a dick. And he did!" That was the first proper coaching lesson I received from Cloughie. To my cost, there were many more to come.

I learned from them quickly, as you had to. But as Forest started the league season of 1988-89, I found myself sitting on the sidelines. As Cloughie had warned, I had to prove I was good enough. He made me and fellow newcomer Garry Parker watch and wait. But it was to prove a memorable first campaign for me, bringing two trips to Wembley finals. Forest finished third in the league behind Arsenal and Liverpool. And we had an FA Cup run which took us through to that ill-fated Hillsborough semi-final against Kenny Dalglish's Anfield squad. No need to say, in looking back at memories bitter and sweet, which had the greatest impact on me. Hillsborough has a chapter on its own later in the book.

The way the season unfolded, there was no hint of the personal drama to come. After a 2-1 defeat at Norwich on the opening day, Forest went on a nine-game unbeaten run. I was looking on and learning. My debut finally came as a substitute in a 3-3 draw at West Ham on November 12th. Cloughie always liked to sit close to a player and I was on the bench next to him. Stuart Pearce, the captain, played a pass that got cut out and West Ham scored. By now, you'll be familiar with the script! I looked at Cloughie and he was staring straight at the centre of the pitch. Then he grabbed my knee tight. "Lawsy, can you play left back?" he said. "Yes gaffer, anything," I replied. "Good, you're on, get ready."

Up went the number 3 card as Cloughie got to his feet. Pearcey looked up from the other side of the field, took off his armband and began a slow walk towards us. Cloughie's patience was wearing thin with Pearcey taking so long walking off. "Come on, hurry up, get off the pitch," he yelled. "Psycho", as he was dubbed, was absolutely glaring as he approached me and I'm thinking "for fuck's sake, Pearcey, don't blame me for this. I've got nothing to do with it." Naturally, I was nervous for another reason, too, because this was my first taste of football in the top flight.

But I kept hearing Cloughie's voice from the sidelines: "Well done, Lawsy, well done. That's the way to play left back." He was doing it deliberately, knowing that it would be winding Pearcey up all the more. At the end of a game, we all knew that if Cloughie had a bee in his bonnet about a particular player then it's him he would be after, no-one else. You could be the worst player on the park but if something else had distracted him then you would get away with it and be delighted. Besides, there was also the entertainment to be had at someone else's expense. When you felt Cloughie would be on the warpath it was always a race to get the best spot in the dressing room for a ringside view.

One thing I learned was never to stare at him when he was giving a bollocking. Better to look down and avoid eye contact because he would be looking round waiting for someone to have a go at. He would murder the first one to raise his head and look at him. Another thing we used to do was roll up a towel and bite on it to make sure we didn't laugh when Cloughie was in full flow, blasting some poor unfortunate team-mate. So it was that we all hurried off Upton Park, thinking: "This is going to be a good one because it's Pearcey – England international, club skipper, Psycho!"

For starters, Pearcey would not sit down in the dressing room. He stood with arms stretched out like metal rods. His fists were clenched and he was staring right through Cloughie. I was wetting myself. Never in all my time at Forest did I see anyone confront the manager like that. Finally Cloughie piped up: "Skipper, do you know why I brought you off?" But Psycho just stood there glaring, never once opening his mouth. He carried on staring. Cloughie said: "Have you ever been punched by a manager?" Still Psycho stood with arms outstretched. We're all thinking: "Oh God, something's really going to kick off here."

Cloughie moved in very quickly with a rabbit punch to Pearcey's stomach. Stuart never so much as flinched as we all held our breath. Then Cloughie took two steps back and said: "You're the nearest thing in football that I can call a friend – and a friend will never hit a friend! You wouldn't hit an old man Stuart, now would you?" At this point, Cloughie stood away. Psycho was still glaring. If looks could kill! I'm sure at that moment Stuart wanted to fight back. But he didn't. He had too much respect for Cloughie. But one thing he insisted on doing was standing his ground. And as we all went for a bath, still Psycho stood there. It was a moment in football that I will never forget.

I'm glad to say I got on well with Pearcey and the relationship continues to this day. To be fair, I got on with most of the players. I was best buddies with Garry Parker and also had a great rapport with Nigel Clough and Gary Crosby. As in all of life, you will always get on better with some people than others. In football, because you are so closely knit, there are bound to be times when you fall out with somebody. That's only human nature. Call it a clash of personalities or whatever you like, but sometimes two people just do not gel. Not that this should make any difference to the way you work professionally.

Now in that Forest dressing room there was one player I could not get along with. His name was Des Walker, the soon-to-be England international centre back who was worshipped by the fans at the City Ground. Des had come through the ranks there as an apprentice and when I arrived he was an established Under-21 international on the verge of a full cap. Somehow I just could not bond with him. I don't know why, but me and him had sparks flying around us from near enough day one.

I didn't like Des and he didn't like me. Sometimes it wasn't even about what was said. It could be something that, if it had come from the mouth of Stuart Pearce or Garry Parker, I'd have laughed off. But if Des Walker said it, I couldn't. I would take it personally. I put up with him for about a year but it was getting to me and something was going to snap. It duly did on a pre-season tour to France. We were in wooden shacks at a training camp near Bordeaux. This was out in the sticks, so we had to do our own thing to entertain ourselves at night. There was a lot of tomfoolery, things like turning over each other's bedrooms.

Mine got done – and straightaway I knew who was responsible. It must have been Des Walker. He'd been eating away at me for so long that I'd had enough and lashed out. I hit Des and knocked him over. I had lost it so badly that I was ready at that moment to go in with a size 10 boot. Thankfully, Mark Crossley jumped on my back to calm me down. He's a big lad, Mark, and he flattened me. I couldn't get up. I think the other lads all knew that something like this was likely to happen at some stage. Des ended up with a fat lip and I cut my hand. But I think it was probably all for the best because it cleared the air between us. We changed towards each other after that.

I should add that Cloughie had not come with us to France. Ronnie Fenton was in charge and, of course, he heard whispers that something had kicked off. The next morning he asked me what had happened. "Nothing really," I said. "And whatever it was, it's been sorted." But I was getting worried because I knew Ronnie would tell the gaffer. Des Walker was a hero at the City Ground and I thought I was heading for deep trouble. To my amazement, nothing was said for weeks . . . until we were having a pre-match meal on an away trip to Norwich.

Cloughie came and sat next to me at the table. He put his hand on my thigh and whispered in my ear: "Did you hit Desmond Walker?" In an equally quiet voice I told him it had all been sorted and that the two of us were alright again. But Cloughie persisted: "I didn't ask you that. I asked you if you had hit Desmond Walker."

By now everybody had stopped eating. I feared I was going to have the kitchen sink thrown at me in front of everyone. "DID YOU HIT DESMOND WALKER?" Cloughie demanded again, this time in a loud voice. "Yes, I did," I said. "Did you hit him HARD?" Cloughie asked. By this time Des had heard what was going on. He stood up and walked out of the dining room, clearly not happy. I wasn't happy, either, because I thought all this had been put behind us and forgotten.

I just said to Cloughie again: "I hit him." Still he wasn't satisfied. "Did you knock his head off," Cloughie went on. "Gaffer, I just hit him," I insisted. "Well, next time KNOCK HIS BLOODY HEAD OFF – AND WELL DONE!" said Cloughie. He kept shouting "well done" and I was just gobsmacked.

Even I can't help but laugh at that story when I tell it again now. But the really important thing is that from that moment onwards I had a much better working relationship with Des. We never socialised much but we got on much better together on the park where we were part of the same Forest defence. That was out of my respect for him as a player and I am sure he had some respect for me as well. He was one of the best defenders in the world at that time.

It was a month later that I made my full First Division debut at right back in a 1-1 draw at Southampton. And I stayed in the side for the rest of the season. Steve Chettle was switched to the centre of the defence, enabling me to take over his number 2 shirt. Garry Parker also made his debut that day at the Dell. The full line-up read: Steve Sutton, myself, Stuart Pearce, Steve Chettle, Colin Foster, Garry Parker, Franz Carr, Neil Webb, Nigel Clough, Lee Chapman and Brian Rice.

After I'd played about half-a-dozen games and was beginning to feel part of the team, I decided to be brave. It was time to take Cloughie up on the words he had told me when I first signed: "Don't start talking to me about more money and a better contract until you have got into MY team." Well, I was in and ready to talk business. But there was another lesson I was still to learn about life at Forest under Cloughie. On the days when he was in a good mood and high humour, you would find no more generous a person. He would do anything for his players. But if he was in a bad mood you would get nothing and you approached him at your peril.

If only I had known then that the players always took the precaution of sounding out Ronnie Fenton on Cloughie's state of mind before making an approach. In I jumped, feet first, with a knock on the manager's door. I was summoned to enter and started by saying: "Gaffer, you remember when I first came here you told me I had to be in your team before I could talk to you about money . . . "

I got no further. Cloughie roared back: "No player tells me when a contract should be improved. You cheeky bastard, I'll pull you when the time is right, not you pull me, that's not the way it works at this club. GET OUT!"

Out I went with a flea in my ear and I knew then that he was going to make me wait for a better contract. And to be fair to him, he was as good as his word! But a valuable lesson had been learned; how and when to try to get the best out of Cloughie. I thought I knew a lot after my spells at Burnley, Huddersfield and Middlesbrough, but I have never met any manager before or since with such an aura about him. He commanded so much respect, not just from people inside football but also outside the game.

Just how highly he was regarded was demonstrated to me at a civic reception staged by Nottingham City Council after we had won the League Cup. It was a noisy do and there must have been about 2,000 people there. Everybody was bubbling and having a good time when suddenly the doors opened and in walked Cloughie, who had not travelled there with us on the bus. Suddenly all heads turned and the room fell silent. I thought: "Wow, that just shows you about this man." Without doubt, he had the respect of everyone who met him. You won't find many people willing to slag off Brian Clough, only those who have not had a very good time with him and even then very few. For all the problems he had in later life, with his drinking and the way it affected his health, no-one has done the dirty on him. And rightly so.

6

Life at Forest: It's Like a Box of Chocolates!

Does anyone remember the Simod Cup? Not many, I'll bet. I do – because Cloughie made it unforgettable. Anyone who followed football closely in those days will recall it better under its nickname of the "Mickey Mouse Cup." Actually, it was called the Full Members Cup when it started in 1985. And the reason it was introduced highlights the one big disappointment for me in my time at Nottingham Forest. I did not get the chance to play in Europe.

Eight years before my arrival at the City Ground, Cloughie had led Forest to the second of two successive European Cup triumphs, beating first Malmo and then Hamburg, each by a single goal. But the tragedy at the Heysel Stadium in 1985, where 39 Juventus fans died at the Italian club's European Cup final against Liverpool, meant that English clubs were banned from international competition. As a result, a new domestic tournament was introduced for clubs in the top two divisions. By 1988-89, my first season in Nottingham, it was known under the sponsored title of the Simod Cup.

Well, we went and won it that year. What's most memorable about it for me is a little scene played out in the background after we had beaten Chelsea 4-1 at Stamford Bridge to get into the quarter-finals where we were drawn away to Ipswich. The point is there was nothing included in our contracts to cover this new competition. It was an opportunity to get to Wembley and the club were reaping the financial rewards. Cloughie just said we would have to negotiate anything that was in it for us. An agreed figure was duly thrashed out in advance of the quarter-final. We won 3-1 at Portman Road and a couple of days later Cloughie summoned us all to the trophy room. He was accompanied by his backroom staff of Liam O'Kane, Archie Gemmill and Graham Lyas, the physio. All three were carrying huge boxes of chocolates.

"The boxes of chocolates are for your wives," said Cloughie. "Or your girlfiends. Or in some cases your boyfriends! And there is a little something for you."

Along with the chocolates came a women's magazine with an envelope attached. We were more than happy and a similar scene was re-enacted after we had won the semi-final. This time we were drawn at home against Crystal Palace. Ian Wright scored for them but we eased through 3-1. So now we were set for a final with Everton who had beaten Queens Park Rangers 1-0 in the other semi-final.

Stuart Pearce raised the question among the players about how much we should get for winning the final and a big meeting took place. It was agreed that he would negotiate for us and that we wanted £10,000 a man. So Stuart padded up and went in to bat, probably knowing a few bouncers would be whistling around his ears. Pearcey did as he was told, with words to the effect of: "We want ten, gaffer. Nothing more, nothing less."

The reaction was predictable. "You cheeky bastard!"

raged Cloughie. "Is that for the lot of you?" Stuart stood his ground. "No, for each of us," he said.

Back came Cloughie: "I can't believe you lot. I'll tell you what I'll do. If you win I'll give you ten. If you lose you give me ten. Deal? Now get out of my office."

It says something for our confidence as a group that when Stuart came back in the dressing room we were more than happy with those terms. In fact, we were rubbing our hands in delight, all looking forward to our ten grand bonus.

We really had to earn it, though. At Wembley in front of just over 46,000 fans – not a bad turn out for a "Mickey Mouse" competition – the score with Everton was 2-2 after 90 minutes. It was a cracker and the supporters got more than their money's worth. The drama continued into extra-time as goals from Garry Parker and Lee Chapman, who scored two each, saw us squeeze to a 4-3 victory.

The trophy was ours and, as you can imagine, we were eagerly anticipating our rewards. There was a chorus of "We're in the money" from our jubilant dressing room. And I'll always remember Des Walker's celebration. He rolled up a wad of money into the shape of a big fat cigar and sat in the bath raising it to his lips and pretending to smoke it. Cloughie walked past in disgust. He was really wound up about it.

Nevertheless, a few days later we were all summoned to the trophy room for that now familiar ceremony involving the chocolates, the magazine and the envelope. But I wondered how any envelope could contain that much money. All sorts of images were flashing through my mind when the chocolate boxes started to appear. Cloughie was yapping away but no-one was interested in what he was saying. There was no sign of a bulging envelope. "Must be a cheque," someone whispered.

Then up piped Cloughie again. "Box of chocolates for your wives, your girlfriends or your boyfriends – and yours is on the back."

We tore open the envelopes and the look on our faces must have been a picture. All we found was a £10 note! Steve Hodge was the first to react. "What's this?" he demanded. "I thought we agreed ten grand." And Cloughie just said: "Now don't you fucking start. That's your money. No-one mentioned ten grand. The figure was 10. We agreed ten and that's what you're getting. Nothing else. Now get out of my sight!"

He'd stung us. Rightly so, perhaps, and fair play to him for slapping us down. I just laughed about it, but one or two others couldn't see the funny side. Steve Hodge was one. He just ripped up his tenner, picked up his chocolates and stormed out.

That was pure Cloughie. Always off the cuff but sharp as a needle with it. You had to learn how to fit in with his ways and I found things difficult when I first got into the Forest team. That's because there was no coaching as such or any functional work that would tell you how to play as a team. I believe now that Brian Clough had a plan early in his managerial career of how he wanted his teams to play. And he slotted players into that plan, sometimes regardless of their ability.

They did not have to be superstars. It was about filling a certain role. I think that's why he went for a lot of players who were relatively unknown and with little more than average ability. But put them in that Forest team and they were much more than average. John McGovern, who lifted those European Cups, is perhaps the readiest example of a player who was made for Cloughie and vice versa. There was this knack for bringing the best out of people. But his teaching tool was not the normal coaching practice with which I was more familiar. It was based around incidents that occurred in games.

Cloughie's philosophy was "learn quick and don't do it again." If you kept making the same mistake you weren't in the side, simple as that. Cloughie would drop you like a stone. Just look at what happened with Stuart Pearce when he was substituted in my debut game at West Ham. What other manager would dream of hauling off his skipper, a seasoned England international at that, just because he had made a bad pass? Cloughie was the only one in the country at that time who had the bollocks to do it. And he was the only manager who could get away with it.

His methods were bizarre but also enlightening. And above all, they worked. Not to mention the dressing room entertainment that was often provided. It was funny, providing you weren't the one on the receiving end, of course. I've mentioned how we would bite on rolled up towels to stop ourselves from laughing.

The manager should have had a degree in sports psychology because there could be no better teacher. Football is now full of so-called psychology experts making a small fortune and thinking they are bringing some new invention to the table. Crap! Cloughie was doing it for years – he just didn't have the title to go with it. As a manager myself, I have been on all the courses and listened to all the hoo-haa, but none of these "experts" can hold a candle to Cloughie. Not only was he the best, he was unique and his methods worked. Okay, he would look aloof at times and come over as strange to people. Sometimes he would make a remark that would make you wonder what on earth he was on about. Then, two or three months down the line, something would happen and suddenly the penny would drop.

Looking back now, after such a slow start at the City Ground, I can hardly believe how eventful my first season there was to become. Forest were Wembley winners twice over, also lifting the League Cup – but only after a huge personal drama that was to lead to as much pain as pleasure. It was the season, too, when Cloughie incurred the wrath of the FA for hitting supporters on the pitch. And, needless to say, there was the anguish of the Hillsborough disaster.

Let's go back first to the start of our great run in the Littlewoods League Cup. We thrashed Chester 10-0 on aggregate in the second round before squeezing past Coventry 3-2 in the third. Then came Leicester City at Filbert Street and after a goalless draw in the first match, we won the replay 2-1 at home in what was my first full appearance in the competition. It seemed we were unstoppable. Come the quarter-final with QPR, we stormed through 5-2 with Lee Chapman scoring four.

The draw favoured us as we were paired with Third Division Bristol City in the semis while West Ham faced Luton. Despite us inevitably being hot favourites, Bristol were no mugs. They had a lot of experience in the side with men like former Everton and Newcastle full-back John Bailey and Steve McClaren, eventually to manage England, in midfield. But the biggest threat to us was posed by Bristol's fearsome Scottish striker Joe Jordan, who was also player-manager at the time.

So it shouldn't be rated a total surprise that Bristol held

us 1-1 in the first leg at the City Ground where only an own goal by John Pender enabled us to travel to the West Country on level terms. Ashton Gate was packed to the rafters with a crowd of over 28,000 sensing an upset. It was just as tight on the field and the tension was such that we reached the 90 minute mark with the game still goalless. Finally, the only goal was grabbed in extra-time by my old room-mate Garry Parker to take us through 2-1 on aggregate.

Although Forest were no strangers to Wembley at that time – having played in three successive League Cup finals between 1978 and 1980 – Nottingham was awash with excitement. Again we were favourites in being pitched against Ray Harford's Luton who were engaged in a battle to preserve their top flight status. We had already beaten Luton 3-2 at Kenilworth Road in the league to make up for a 0-0 draw against them at the City Ground.

This was going to be my first ever experience of playing at Wembley. It was what I had dreamed about since I was a small boy kicking a ball about with my mates back in Wallsend. I had never even been to Wembley, let alone played there. To see those famous twin towers and then to play beneath them was going to be the biggest day of my life. But then, just 10 days before the final, a freak accident at home left me shattered.

It happened while performing the sort of task all of us do nearly every day. I was in the kitchen holding some glasses which I was putting away in a cupboard. I tripped over and one of the glasses broke. Yet I never felt a thing. Certainly, there was no way I could imagine the damage I'd done. But the warning sign was to see blood spurting from a finger. Although I still couldn't feel anything, it was like water coming out of a pistol.

Evidently, I had hit an artery and blood was everywhere. It splashed on the cupboards, the walls and the floor. I was in shock and didn't know what to do. My wife Margaret rang straightaway for an ambulance and wrapped a towel tight around my hand while we waited. Even as I travelled to Nottingham's Queen's Medical Centre, I was thinking that just a few stitches would put me right. I should have known better, of course, because the towel was just soaked in blood. As soon as they took it off for a look in the casualty department, the wound started pumping again. And I knew from the way they were talking that something was seriously wrong.

There was talk of getting a surgeon to see me fast. Apparently, I needed micro-surgery. Not surprising really considering my hand was a dreadful mess with so much skin hanging off that you could see the bone of my thumb. But footballers can be blind to the consequences, especially with a Wembley final less than a fortnight away. I still thought to myself that I would be going straight home once they had cleaned me up and put in some stitches. It was only when I was told that I would have to stay in overnight that the doubts began to surface.

"Will I be alright for the League Cup final?" I asked. They fobbed me off, saying they would discuss that later after the surgeon had finished with me. I was knocked out for the micro-surgery and sent straight through to the operating theatre.

When I came round something was clearly missing. I couldn't see my hand. Where was it? Finally, through a haze, I saw it raised in the air. There was a pot on my wrist and my fingers were supported by a network of wires.

What a shocking sight. My heart just sank. The surgeon explained that he had needed to put 40-odd stitches inside my hand. It had been a real mess. And he warned me that I might even lose the feeling in my thumb and the finger next to it.

I took in everything he said but there was only one thing I wanted to know. "Just tell me, can I play in the final?" I asked. "Absolutely not," came the reply. Even then, half of me thought he was joking. "Seriously?" I said. "Seriously," he insisted. "And if you do try to play you could lose the use of your finger and thumb."

My emotions were in turmoil. I was panicking. "Well, chop them off then," I said. "Do anything. I don't care. I'm not missing this final. It might be the only chance I get to play at Wembley." Naturally, the surgeon ignored the outburst and settled me down. Then another horrifying truth dawned on me. This was the weekend before the final. Oh shit, what was Cloughie going to say?

After being allowed to leave the hospital, I went into the club on the Monday afternoon of Wembley week still with this pot on and wire sticking out of my fingers. Ronnie Fenton took one look at me and said: "What've you done? Well, that's you bollocksed for the final, isn't it!" I asked if I could go and see the gaffer. When I entered Cloughie's office he was sitting at his desk with his glasses on. After hearing my account, he roared: "You idiot." Then, after a pause: "Are you going to be fit for Sunday?"

Without hesitation, I replied: "Yes boss, of course I am." However, Ronnie Fenton was not so convinced. "Of course, he's not," said Ronnie. "How's he going to play with that? Look at him, he's got a plaster all over his hand."

Cloughie looked straight back at me. "Now I'm asking

you the question," he said. "Can you throw a ball and will you be fit for Sunday?" It was the moment of truth for me. "Yes, I will, I promise," I declared. "Right," boomed Cloughie. "Now get out of my office and get yourself sorted out."

All that week while the rest of the team were preparing for the final, I couldn't train. I couldn't even run because of the jarring effect. The urge was to take everything off my hand and join in. Eventually I did and went to see the club physio to ask his advice. The hand was throbbing, a bit like when you've got toothache. I went for a jog just to see how it would feel, but every time I took a step it was throb, throb, throb. That was when I knew that I really was struggling to make the final. The pain was such that I was not even able to sleep properly.

Despite all this, I did some more light jogging and started kicking a ball from a standing position. "Are you going to be all right?" Cloughie again demanded to know. Once more, I insisted that I would be. But to have any chance at all there was one thing I had to do. I went back to the hospital and saw the surgeon who did the operation. "I need to be able to take a throw-in," I told him. But he was still advising me not to play. He said: "If you go down on your hand in a challenge, you could undo all the good work we've done with the micro-surgery and run the real risk of losing your thumb or finger."

This, though, wasn't something I didn't already know. "I'm prepared to take that risk," I said. "I just want to play in the final. Can you help me?" He knew there was no point in continually trying to put me off and devised a plan. He stitched the tips of my thumb and finger together, inserting a piece of tubing in between to protect the wound.

By now we had got to Thursday and the clock was ticking. I went for a run and could still feel pain, but it was definitely easing a bit. Cloughie saw me and threw a ball to me. "Go on, throw it down the line," he said. Every moment I was touching the ball it was killing me, but somehow I did manage to do the necessary. I did throw the ball down the line. "Good, you're playing," he said, before walking away. I should have been delighted. Underneath, though, I was still panicking and wondered if they could give me an injection to numb the pain.

You won't be surprised to learn that the night before the game I could not sleep, still worrying about my hand and wondering if I would make a dick of myself. Could I really get through 90 minutes at Wembley? Or had I denied somebody else a place in the team? But as the team coach arrived at Wembley, those doubts evaporated. The adrenaline in my body was a powerful painkiller, more than enough to get me through without any further thought of an injection.

I duly played in that final with the plastic tubing between thumb and finger, all strapped up with a skin coloured bandage to make it less obvious that I had a problem. My team-mates all knew, of course, but the opposition didn't.

Came the time for us to leave the dressing room and march up the tunnel. My dream WAS coming true and I was on such a high that I completely forgot about my hand as this tidal wave of noise from the fans hit us full in the face. We had our normal white shorts on and whether it was nerves or not, I was wetting myself as we walked on to the pitch. Not a lot but enough to make for an undignified spectacle. So, far from worrying about my hand, my biggest fear was that the television cameras would capture my embarrassment.

It all seemed so unreal. And once the game started I never gave a thought to my hand from first minute to last. We beat Luton 3-1 with Nigel Clough scoring twice, including a penalty, and Neil Webb getting the other goal. It was only as the game finished, with the job done, that the reality of the odds I'd defied bit back. The pain in my hand returned with a vengeance and I was in agony. I'm sure there must have been twinges during the game, but I never felt a thing because I was so wound up.

It was certainly throbbing as we climbed the steps to lift the cup and get our medals. Weirdly, I can remember thinking that the strapping on my hand had created a little pouch between finger and thumb that was just big enough to fit a medal. The Forest fans had been throwing hats and scarves in our direction for us to wear. Somehow or other I also managed to pick up a banana. And I walked up to the royal box to receive my medal shaking hands with one hand and holding this banana in the other. It was a great, great day for Forest and a great, great day for me. It was the first thing I had won in my career and you just cannot describe the feeling of euphoria when that happens. I am sure that players who have turned out at Wembley many times will all tell you that the first was something special. It certainly was for me. I felt a million dollars.

7

Hillsborough

April 15th, 1989. A date frozen in time forever. And my freeze-frame of that warm, sunny spring afternoon is of preparing to take a throw-in. It was around 3.04pm on the day of what was to become the biggest disaster in British football history.

As I picked up the ball to take that throw early in Nottingham Forest's FA Cup semi-final with Liverpool at Hillsborough, everything was relatively normal. Or so it seemed. It had been a predictably tense start to a hugely important game of football. But I was never to take that throw-in. And the enormity of what followed made the football side of the occasion entirely irrelevant. It became momentous for the worst possible reason; the crowd crush that was to cause the deaths of 96 Liverpool supporters at the Leppings Lane end of the stadium.

I was facing in that direction on the right-hand touchline as the first supporters spilled on to the pitch. Yet scenes like that were not exactly unusual and were almost always connected with crowd trouble. So initially there was only irritation from the players about the hold-up. No-one could possibly have imagined what was actually happening on those packed terraces.

But let's go back a few days because there had been

arguments before the game about which end of the ground the two sets of fans should have. Liverpool, who had the bigger supporter base, were put in the smaller Leppings Lane end. Our fans were given the bigger home end, the Sheffield Wednesday kop. You could understand Liverpool's argument against that, but the decision was based on the geography of the situation. Fans were given the end of Hillsborough nearest to the direction from which they would approach. Routes over the Pennines from Liverpool led naturally to Leppings Lane whereas our supporters coming north would be funnelled towards the other end at Penistone Road.

We travelled up from Nottingham in confident mood. Justifiably so because we hadn't conceded a goal in the competition up to that point. Ipswich and Leeds were both dispatched from the City Ground, beaten 3-0 and 2-0 respectively. Then we won 3-0 at Watford where I managed to get on to the scoresheet with a left-foot screamer. That took us to Old Trafford in the quarter-finals and, in order to demonstrate the air of normality which prevailed before Hillsborough, I make no apologies for detailing the football side of a run that was to be almost obliterated – and understandably so – by the horrendous sequel to it all.

Alex Ferguson had been in charge of Manchester United for three years but was still chasing his first trophy for the club. It was a big, big game for both of us and we knew Cloughie was desperate for us to beat United. Even by his standards, something very odd happened in the dressing room beforehand. Whether it was deliberate or accidental, I don't know to this day. But I think he sensed a bit more nervousness than usual as we sat waiting for kick-off time to approach. And I've already described how Cloughie did everything possible to get us relaxed.

Anyway, I don't know whether he had a drink inside him or not, but his face was distinctly blotchy and red. This, by the way, was well before the days of the well documented problems that got the better of him later. Suddenly Cloughie stood up and said to our physio Graham Lyas: "Have you got any cream for my big head?" Graham pointed him to a table that was full of all kinds of stuff. Cloughie went over, picked up this tube and squirted cream all over his head. Then he rubbed it into his face. It looked like a scene from Mrs Doubtfire – and this is five minutes before a massive match.

Cloughie evidently came to the same realisation and started talking to us. "Right," he said. "This is a big game and I want to beat these . . . "

There he stopped and in that same split-second he began to panic. "Graham," he yelled at the physio. "Why is my face burning?"

Graham went over to the table and quickly found the answer. "Oh no gaffer, you've put deep heat on your face," he said. "What?" spluttered Cloughie. "Well, get it off quick, get it off!" All the lads were trying not to laugh but inwardly we were pissing ourselves. Whether this scene was by accident or design – and I believe it was the latter – it certainly relieved all the tension.

We ran out on to Old Trafford laughing our heads off. It's very hard to laugh before a game because football's such a serious business. But that day we were hysterical and the Manchester United players – Bryan Robson, Gordon Strachan, Mark Hughes and all – were looking at us wondering what the hell was happening.

It worked. We won 1-0 with Garry Parker getting the

vital goal. They say that laughter and tears are so closely related that they are at the same end of the emotional spectrum. We were to experience both in quick succession considering the terrible tragedy that was to unfold after our quarter-final win.

On the journey to Hillsborough, the mood of all of us was to win again for Cloughie. He inspired that in you. We were desperate to do it for him because we knew this was the one domestic competition he had failed to win as a manager. And we were equally aware that the winners of this game would have a great chance to lift the cup in being pitched against either Everton or Norwich in the final. But that day it was Cloughie more than anyone who couldn't give a damn about winning or losing. Or even playing a game of football.

What unfolded was the most chilling contrast with the glorious weather and the setting. Hillsborough was a majestic spectacle as always, even more so in the sunshine. And the pitch, too, was immaculate as we walked out to inspect it. The ground already looked pretty packed an hour before kick-off, the atmosphere was building . . . everything seemed perfect for a cracking semi-final.

And so the game started with us kicking towards the Liverpool fans, half of them in the upper deck seating and the other half crammed into the seething terraces below. Within two minutes of the kick-off we had a stroke of good fortune when Peter Beardsley rattled our crossbar at the Penistone Road end. Game on, we thought.

But just a few minutes later we got the first inkling that something was not right as I prepared to take a throw-in down near the Leppings Lane end. I had the ball in my hand and I was about to throw it towards Nigel Clough, who had come running across the pitch to create space, when suddenly one or two fans ran on to the pitch.

Looking back, I'm mortified about my initial reaction, even though it would have been fully understandable in normal circumstances. In fact, the players' thoughts were one and the same: "You bastards, get off the pitch and let us get on with the game." We assumed they were just idiots and we started swearing at them. But then two or three more fans appeared on the pitch. Then it was five, six and seven. Ever more supporters spilled on to the playing surface, screaming and shouting hysterically.

Slowly we realised these were not hooligans. They were not threatening us, there was real fear in their eyes. We began to suspect something had happened but did not know what. It was all a mystery. At 3.06pm, the official time that the disaster was recorded, referee Ray Lewis took us off the field and back to the dressing rooms. There, we were in suspended animation. It was all about trying to stay focused on the game because even then we had no idea of the seriousness of the situation. Cloughie was sitting on the floor with his legs out, telling us to keep our minds on the job.

Then, several minutes later, referee Lewis came in and said he would try to get us back out on to the pitch as soon as he could. "Well, bloody hurry up about it then," growled Cloughie. We took off our boots and were trying to stay relaxed when in came a police inspector.

"Look," he said. "There is a problem. But we are hoping to restart the game. We think there may have been a fatality. Someone may have been crushed to death."

That was stunning news, however ridiculously understated the policeman's assessment now seems.

Cloughie was first to react. "What?" he said. "Someone's been killed? Then that's it. Game off. We're going home. The game means sod all now."

But that was evidently not what the police inspector wanted to hear. "No, no, you can't do that," he insisted. "It's not my decision and it's not your decision. We ARE going to try and restart the game."

"Not with me you're not," growled Cloughie. Then someone else entered the dressing room and said that three or four people had been killed. Suddenly, the realisation dawned that a major disaster was unfolding.

"Well, you'd better abandon the game because we're not going back on, forget it," repeated Cloughie. "Lads, get changed." The mood had changed so much that a personal form of panic set in. We all had our families at the game. They were out in the stands, quite safe as it turned out. But we were so much in the dark about what had happened that we wanted to make sure they were all right.

My wife was in the crowd, so was my six-year-old daughter and five-year-old son. Were they okay? Had the trouble spilled over to where they were sitting? We didn't have any answers to our fears, so we got changed quickly. I made my way out on to the pitch to find my family and to discover just what the hell was going on. And what I found was like a scene from some horror film. It was just so unreal.

Amid a deathly silence, there were bodies lying on advertising boards. I was choked. It was frightening to see. But I still had to find my family and make sure they were safe. Eventually I did, to my great relief. We were then ushered up into some rooms with the instruction to keep out of the way and let the emergency services do what they could to help the injured and dying.

Almost every minute that went by, the death toll got higher and higher. First it was 40, then 50 and 60. Still it did not stop. Even as we watched the scenes on television, it was difficult to take in just what had happened. But it hit us hard.

It might have been Liverpool fans who were the victims, but we at Nottingham Forest felt acutely for them. Football just then did not matter. After all, it's only kicking a bag of wind around. And we felt sure that the FA Cup competition that season would be abandoned along with the game itself.

On the journey back to the City Ground, Cloughie, too, was in shock. Nobody knew quite what to do or what to say. It was the quietest bus journey that I have ever known. Everyone just stared out of the window. When we got home and switched the television on, Hillsborough was still filling the screens. I thought the best and only way of dealing with it was to shut yourself down.

This cloud of disbelief hung over us as we reported back for training a couple of days later. We still had no idea what was going to happen. Would the game be played again or not? Finally, with Everton already waiting in the final, news came through of the FA's decision. Our semi-final was to be replayed at Old Trafford on May 7th, 22 days after Hillsborough.

By then, funeral services had been held throughout Merseyside. The formal period of mourning was over – but when we got back to football business with Liverpool we knew that the whole of English football would only want to see one winner. Apart from us, of course, and it was only natural if we were a little sheepish about our hopes. There was a huge tidal wave of sympathy and emotion behind the Liverpool team and their fans. It was a no-win situation for us because nobody outside Nottingham wanted to see Forest in the final. Even if we did win, everybody would claim that Liverpool's hearts had not been in the game.

Of course, things were far more difficult for them. But no-one should think we didn't share their trauma. When I watched a documentary about Hillsborough 10 years after the event, I cried my eyes out. I could not believe I would still be that choked. I know the police have been heavily criticised for the way they handled the situation – and rightly so – but I do think some of the Liverpool fans also have to take their share of the blame for what happened that day. Despite all the warnings beforehand, some turned up late and others arrived without tickets, still wanting to be part of the action. When the gate outside the Leppings Lane end was opened, in they charged. I still feel that the tragedy would not have happened if those without tickets had stayed away. This is without any disrespect or lack of sympathy for the loss Liverpool felt as a city, particularly the families of lost loved ones to whom my heart goes out to this day.

As you can well imagine, the replay was a highly-charged occasion for everyone involved and not for the reasons normally associated with a big game of football. And yet, once we had paid our respects to those fans who died, it was a REAL game that developed. We wanted to win it and so did they. Even then, with the weight of feeling of the nation against us, we knew we would have to pull out an extraordinary performance to do it.

We tried our very best but it was not to be, even though we hauled ourselves level with a goal from Neil Webb after

John Aldridge had put Liverpool in front. After half-time Aldridge struck again. Then I got on the scoresheet – at the wrong end!

The own goal was bad enough, what hurt even more was the way Aldridge twisted the knife. It was his gesture after I put the ball into my own net that became the big talking point and a subject of petty controversy that this, of all games, could have done without.

I remember a cross coming in from the right which swung deep towards the far post. Aldridge was going for it but I got in there first. It was the sort of situation I would deal with easily 99 times out of 100. But on this occasion I didn't, partly because of the worn-out Old Trafford pitch. As I was leading with my left foot to clear the ball, it hit a divot, diverted against the side of my leg and looped into the corner of the net beyond goalkeeper Steve Sutton. At that moment, I just sank to my knees, I was devastated. You don't want to be scoring an own goal at any time, let alone in an FA Cup semi-final.

But, of course, it had to be kept in context with all that had happened previously. That's why I felt there was no excuse for the fact that Aldridge just could not help himself from taking the mick. Despite the tragic events of three weeks earlier, he came up to me and ruffled my hair. At first I did not know it was him. But when I looked up and saw Aldridge, I also saw the expression on the faces of my Forest team-mates. They were furious with him. Angry that, after everything, he had shown no respect. And that hurt me, too. Even more, in fact. I took it personally. It was unforgivable for Aldridge to have done that. And there was a lot made of it in the press and on television.

As it turned out, I didn't have long to wait to try to get

my revenge. Just three days later we travelled to Anfield to play Liverpool in a league game. When the team coach arrived Aldridge was actually waiting to attempt an apology to me. But I was having none of that. I told him: "Fuck off. You've done the damage, I'll see you on the park." Stuart Pearce then pushed me past Aldridge and into our dressing room.

Nobody was a greater upholder of fair play than Brian Clough. Yet feelings were running so high that before kick-off Cloughie told me that it would not bother him if I got sent off. At this point let me tell you I've been dismissed in my career for things I haven't meant. This time, could I get my marching orders? Could I hell as like! Despite having the manager's blessing, I just could not nail Aldridge. I followed him all over the pitch. He knew what was happening and I suspect the referee did, too. I reckon he might have turned a blind eye to what I was trying to do. But Aldo rode all my tackles and challenges and I simply couldn't get to him.

Since that time, the pair of us have been fellow managers and were able to put our differences behind us. We even met on holiday once and spoke about what happened in that replay. I know now that he regrets what he did. He apologised again; we kissed and made up. Although we're not exactly mates, we can get on with each other. The years of hatred are behind us – and it really was hatred on my part. But I confess I was satisfied when eventually I did manage to get a little slice of revenge on Aldridge – as you'll discover in a later chapter.

8

Bring me Sunshine . . .

But for my own goal we might have gone to Wembley THREE times in my first season at Forest. But what an extraordinary year it was. A powerful mixture of triumph and tragedy. The fulfilment of dreams and some scenes that will haunt me forever.

They say that when you have tasted something once then you want it all the more. Those who have never played at Wembley don't know what it's like and don't realise what they are missing. Those who have done so simply get hooked on the sensation. In a strange sort of way they have more to lose. I'm happy to say that at Forest the addiction and the craving kept being satisfied. Wembley became a second home to us over the next few seasons and I was there five times in all. Less than 12 months after winning the League Cup and Simod Cup we were back there once more, again in the Littlewoods competition. This time our opponents were Joe Royle's Oldham Athletic and Nigel Jemson scored the only goal of the game to help us retain the trophy. So . . . three appearances at Wembley, three victories. I had yet to know the feeling of being a Wembley loser. It was to come, unfortunately. I was happy to wait.

Something else I had to wait for was a nickname at the City Ground. But then again I'd never had one at any of my three previous clubs. It was always "Lawsy" and I was happy enough to have it left at that. I had been at Forest for almost a full season when all of a sudden they started calling me . . . Ernie!

I was puzzled. But at first I never questioned it because I thought: "Well, that's not very hurtful. I'll have it, I can handle that." It would be "Ernie" Laws this and "Ernie" Laws that. And I'm left trying to work out why. It was Steve Chettle who first gave me the handle and gradually all the rest followed suit. I answered to it and got used to it, still without a clue as to what inspired it.

Eventually curiosity got the better of me and I had to find out. "Go on then, tell me," I said. "Ernie Wise!" came the reply. I was stunned. Why on earth was that? Was it because all the young lads came up to me for advice and thought I was the "wise" one? If so, I'd be pretty pleased about that.

But my illusions were soon shattered. "It's because of your short, fat hairy legs – and you wear a wig!" my team-mates insisted. Now first of all let me say my barnet used to look exactly the same whether it was before a game or just after it. I could have played 90 minutes and been sweating buckets and yet my hair would look exactly the same. It was wiry and never moved. Not my fault, I was born with it. But the players thought that because it never moved, it must be a wig! As for the short, fat hairy legs, I reckoned I had to live with that.

Anyway, the nickname has stuck with me and whenever I see my mate Pearcey or one of the others from that squad they always greet me with: "Hi Ernie, how're you doin'" It's a nickname I now regard with some affection. Cloughie always used to call me by it as well. I recall a dressing room scene at Wembley before the 1991 FA Cup final against Tottenham. Cloughie had this suit on and was wearing a big red rosette that had on it the words "The World's Greatest Grandad." Unusually, I think he was nervous and he was looking at himself in the mirror.

"Skipper?" he called. "Who's the fashion guru of this dressing room? How do I look?" Pearcey turned round and said: "Gaffer, Ernie's the man you should be asking." Now I knew Pearcey was really taking the mick because most of the lads would be wearing their designer shirts while I would be kitted out by Marks and Spencer. My North East upbringing would not allow me to pay out for the latest trendy fashion when I could get at least two shirts for the price of their one. In fact, Pearcey always said I should wear a flat cap, a short-sleeved shirt and a waistcoat with some fags shoved up my sleeve.

So Cloughie turned to me and said: "Ernie, is it right that you are the fashion king? Well, what do you think of your manager now?" I told him: "Gaffer, you look a million dollars. But I must say before you walk out there is one thing."

Cloughie looked at me quizzically wondering how I could possibly pick fault with what he was wearing. In turn, I knew he could be a bit eccentric but I didn't think even he could be as daft as this. You see, he hadn't considered his footwear. Looking him up and down, I said: "You look great – but I'd get rid of the slippers!"

He looked down and to his horror found he'd still got his brown slippers on. He was all set to walk out at Wembley – in his slippers – to meet Princess Diana! Can you imagine the field day the media would have had with that? "God almighty, thanks son – I would have walked out in those as well," said a grateful Cloughie.

Of course, what he *really* wanted to wear was that old green jersey he always had on at every game. So Cloughie handed it to one of the young apprentices and told him he would give him a bonus if he carried this jersey out on to the field – so he could change into it after the formal introductions. This young lad was not in the team but suddenly found himself walking out with us at Wembley to meet Princess Diana, carrying this bloody green jersey!

It was a great honour for me to meet Princess Di. She was fantastic and this was something special in my life. It was not just her stunning looks but the aura she had about her. I am a very patriotic person and I have to say I shed some tears after she died in that tragic car accident in Paris. I still have a framed photograph of me shaking hands with Princess Di before that Wembley game. I used to have it hanging in my manager's office at Scunthorpe United. But the day itself was more bitter than sweet. In fact, a sad day all round. For starters, I was left out of Forest's FA Cup final line-up and only made the bench. There were three of us in the same boat. Steve Hodge and myself would be subs while Nigel Jemson learned he didn't even have a place on the bench.

Any player will tell you it is tough being dropped for any match, let alone a final. For me, it was a particularly nasty surprise. I had played in the majority of games leading up to the final. And it had been a long haul. We needed three attempts to scrape past Crystal Palace in the third round and also needed replays in rounds four and five to edge out Newcastle and Southampton. Finally we had a win at the first attempt in beating Norwich 1-0 in the quarter-finals before breezing past West Ham 4-0 in the semis. Frankly, I expected to be in the side to play Tottenham in the final. I learned of Cloughie's decision while we were locked away in a hotel down south preparing for the game and felt I deserved to know my fate in a far more respectful manner.

It was the Friday, just 24 hours ahead of the game, and we'd had a five-a-side. Afterwards I saw Cloughie hand Stuart Pearce a crumpled up little piece of paper. Written on it was the team. Cloughie then got in a car and left the training ground, leaving Pearcey to tell us who was playing. We all got back on the bus to return to the hotel. Once there, Pearcey stood up and said: "Right lads, here's the team." He unravelled this bit of paper and reeled off the names. When he got to number 11 my name had not been called out. Instead, I was included as one of the substitutes. And Gary Charles was going to play in my position at right back.

"Pearcey, stop taking the piss," I said. But he said deadpan: "That's the team. If you've got a problem go and see the gaffer." Well, I DID have a problem. I was fuming. This was no ordinary game. It was an FA Cup final. And to be told in this manner that I wasn't playing was, in my opinion, way out of order. I went in search of Cloughie but couldn't find him. I suppose he knew I was going to be unhappy, along with others, and stayed out of the way. He didn't want a confrontation.

What wound me up even more was that Gary Charles was carrying a hamstring injury. I knew he would not last the game at Wembley. It annoyed me that Gary should have been more honest about that. Then again, I had taken a risk with my hand in the 1989 League Cup final and it's always hard for the player to make a judgment on himself. Still, I felt Gary should have come clean. Cloughie might not have known but all the lads knew full well that Gary was struggling. I struggled, too, to feel part of it at Wembley as the game kicked off with me sitting disconsolately on the bench.

But my mind was quickly taken off my disappointment. The first incident of the game saw Paul Gascoigne go straight through Paul Parker and stud him right in the stomach. Gascoigne should have been booked at least. Gazza was by now an experienced player, a key member of the England squad who had played in the previous year's World Cup finals in Italy. But he was always highly-strung and you could see he was really wound up for this final.

We were playing well, starting the game brightly to take the upper hand. Gazza was chasing around looking as if he wanted to kick anything that moved. He managed it again well inside the quarter-hour mark when Gary Charles broke forward to the edge of the box. There he was halted by an horrendous tackle from Gascoigne. Ironically, it was Gazza who was hurt the most and was stretchered off. Obviously we didn't know the extent of it then, but it proved to be cruciate ligament damage that would keep him out of football for a long time.

From the free-kick Gazza left behind him on the Wembley pitch, Stuart Pearce smashed the ball into the net to put Forest 1-0 up. My personal anguish was fleetingly forgotten. We were all jumping up and down on the bench. All, that is, except for Cloughie. I was right next to him and he just sat there, staring straight out into the middle of the pitch. And this was the FA Cup final, the one domestic honour that had eluded him. Yet he never seemed to watch that free-kick and never showed one bit of emotion when it flew in.

Now I don't know whether that was because he knew the media would be looking at him with a camera pointing in his direction from every angle, and he didn't want to show his feelings. But one thing I do know is that I couldn't have done it. As a manager myself, I get so excited, even in an ordinary league game. For Cloughie to act the way he did that day was bizarre, even by his standards.

Had he been drinking? I don't know, I can't say that. I know he had started taking drink by then but it was something he kept well hidden from the players. Only those close to him knew the true extent. Most strange of all about Cloughie that day was his reaction at the end of 90 minutes after Spurs had equalised to force extra time. The players were out on the pitch and I was there with them, handing out drinks and trying to encourage them. This was the time they needed some inspiration from the manager. But he just sat there. He would not even come off the bench where he was the only one left sitting there. All the coaching staff were trying to rally the troops, but there he sat.

Much as I loved playing for Cloughie and owe him so much, that, to me, was a big mistake. When his team needed him the most he was not there for them. I am sure when he looked back that he must have regretted it. This was his best chance of winning the FA Cup. Instead, it was Terry Venables who was out there on the Wembley pitch lifting his Tottenham side to go on and win 2-1 after an own-goal from Des Walker. Charles was beginning to struggle with his hamstring injury and I was sat there next to Cloughie, saying: "Come on, get me on." Finally he did and I played some part at least in what was to be my first and only experience of an FA Cup final. It was the only time I experienced defeat in five visits to Wembley – and it was a horrible taste.

I was already sulking at being left out of the side and then we were beaten. To this day I still feel we would have won had myself and Steve Hodge been in the team from the start. And with Nigel Jemson left on the bench! Being serious, my mind went back to an incident after our League Cup triumph earlier that season. It was amusing, but maybe a harmless prank that backfired in some way. It happened while we were parading the trophy in an open top bus in the centre of Nottingham. I felt privileged to be up there being cheered by adoring supporters and to have my son and daughter by my side. Amidst all that, and with Cloughie right there with us, Nigel Jemson bent down and whispered something in the ear of my then four-year-old son. As we all know, young kids repeat what they are told – and what my lad was told was this: "Cloughie, you are a wanker!" Sure enough, the words came out. Cloughie heard it, turned and said: "I know who said that." He was staring right at me, but through me – at Jemson. "It was you, you little shit!" he said.

For all the later disappointment back at Wembley, I have still got my loser's medal. But it's in a box in my garage. I never look at it because I never felt I earned it. The only thing I remember with pride is being presented to Princess Di. Everything else about the day upsets me even now. I just felt it was garbage the way I was treated. When I did finally get a showdown with Cloughie his reaction was simply this: "I'm the manager, I pick the team." That was his only answer, but then no matter what else he might have said, it would not have made me feel any better.

9

Don't Shoot the Messenger. Or Mess with Keano!

Life under Cloughie was never dull. How could it be? In fact, it sounds like an understatement to say it like that. I knew he was different, but just how different became clear to me at a very early stage. And it had nothing to do with the football. After my first pre-season tour with Forest we had just landed back at East Midlands airport when Cloughie grabbed my shoulder and said: "Lawsy, give this to my brother."

He handed me a bottle of whisky and a big wad of money – and then walked off. I was left standing there just outside the baggage section wondering what the hell to do. I didn't know Brian Clough had a brother, let alone where to find him. Fortunately, Nigel Clough was still around. "A package for Uncle Joe?" he asked. "Ah yes, he lives in Middlesbrough."

It seems Cloughie had automatically thought that because I was still a Middlesbrough resident at the time I would obviously know where his family lived. It's a bit like when you meet people from the same town or city on holiday abroad and you get that ridiculous feeling that you must have met them before – forgetting that they are one of hundreds of thousands of people living in that place. Cloughie must have thought: "Middlesbrough's not that large a place. He'll know where to find them."

Anyway, Nigel gave me Joe's telephone number so I could call him for directions to the house. When I rang I got a bit of a shock. For a moment, I honestly thought it was Cloughie himself on the other end of the line. The voice sounded just like him. But I was to discover that there the similarity ended. When I found the house and knocked on the door, Uncle Joe did not look much like Brian at all.

Feeling rather embarrassed, I gave him the bottle of whisky and the money which I had wrapped in a brown paper envelope. There must have been about £500 – quite a lot of cash in those days. Joe then asked me where I had parked my car and told me to back it on to his drive. Without finding out why, I did as he requested. I was still sitting in the car when he said: "Open your boot." From that moment, I kept hearing thud, thud, thud. Something quite heavy – and quite a lot of it – was being put into the boot. I just sat still, not wanting to look or to ask.

But my imagination was running wild. What on earth was it? Once I had left Uncle Joe and rounded the corner out of sight of the house, I couldn't resist stopping to have a look. What I found was six bags of spuds! They came back with me to Nottingham and were still in the boot when I reported for training on the following Monday morning.

Cloughie came to find me. "Lawsy, have you got something for me?" he said. So we went to his car to complete the delivery of the spuds, which I presume Joe had grown himself. "These are the best you will ever get," insisted Cloughie. I thought to myself: Yes, and they must also be the most expensive! Cloughie then gave me a spud – just one, mind – with the words: "Here, have one yourself."

Anyway, from then on I was used as the delivery man between the brothers. It even got to the point where Cloughie would lend me his own big Mercedes and tell me I could use it over the weekend . . . just so long as I brought back whatever stuff his brother had to give him. I remember the car had a phone in it, which was extremely rare at that time. I have to say I did enjoy myself cruising in Cloughie's car, though I dare not abuse the privilege for fear of getting my arse kicked.

All this had been going on for some time when Cloughie used me as the butt of a joke at a testimonial dinner for goalkeeper Steve Sutton. All the players were booked to sit on separate tables with the various companies who were sponsoring the dinner, at which Cloughie was due to give his first speech in public for about five years.

For a supposedly extrovert character he looked quite nervous. When he saw me standing in the foyer he came up and asked: "Brian, where are you sitting?" I told him I was somewhere near the back. "No you aren't," he said. "You're sitting with me on the top table. You're keeping me company."

I protested that I couldn't do that because it was Steve Sutton's night, not mine. But Cloughie wouldn't hear of it. "I'm telling you, you're sitting with me," he insisted. I felt really sheepish about that but Steve told me not to worry and just do what the gaffer wanted. So I sat up there with him, the pair of us chatting away.

Finally, up stood Cloughie to make his speech. A little way in, he suddenly turned to me and said: "People don't realise, I only bought him as a postman!" I was sat there thinking: "Well, that's one hell of an expensive postman you bought yourself, gaffer!" I know he was only joking – well, at least I thought he was! You could never quite tell with Cloughie, an absolute one-off.

The only one at the club who really knew him was Nigel Clough, his son. Nigel still lived at home with his parents, but he always came to work separately from his father. "Morning Nigel," Cloughie would say. And Nigel would completely ignore him! He was good at hiding his feelings for his dad, so good that the rest of us could talk about Cloughie, as all players do about their managers, and know that Nigel wouldn't react. We also knew he wouldn't go off telling tales, which tells you something about the relationship that existed between Nigel and the rest of the lads, and the respect we had for him. I doubt I could have been like him. If someone was saying things in front of me about my father, I'm sure I'd lash out.

But Nigel just got on with it. He was no "daddy's boy" and was accepted as just one of the lads. Strangely, it was me rather than Nigel who would get wound up if I heard someone slagging off Cloughie, particularly if it was a player he had brought to Forest from the obscurity of reserve team football or the lower divisions. That was not on in my book, he didn't deserve that. He had given them their chance and that was no way to repay him. Other than that, I've always believed that the dressing room is a place where players should be allowed to have a gripe among themselves. It's their domain. As a manager myself, I'm never bothered by the thought that players will be having a moan about me, calling me this and that. It's human nature. We all talk about our bosses. A lot if it is heat of the moment stuff and not really meant. For footballers, it's a safety valve to let off steam about their manager.

Another way of doing that is in activities outside football, bonding sessions aimed at bringing everyone together. I found I was quite good at organising things for the team and was appointed entertainments officer by my Forest colleagues. To me, team spirit was paramount and I was always wanting us to do things as a group. Togetherness was the key to our success at Forest. If we went out on a Saturday night we would often meet up as a group with our wives and girlfriends. We had parties at each other's houses and all stuck together. It wasn't Cloughie who created the spirit in the dressing room, it was the players and the fact that we got on well with each other.

When it came to getting away from the club, I always wanted us to be adventurous. One thing I organised was paintballing. It was billed as Forest v Notts County. We got kitted up in all the gear, armed with these big guns that fire balls of paint rather than bullets. But let me tell you it still hurts when you get hit.

In the first game it was our job to protect an important canister as the County lads came up over a hill to attack us. If you got hit, you were out of the game and were supposed to walk out of the zone with your hands up. We were like bloody schoolkids, as you can imagine. Stuart Pearce and myself were on guard duty and suddenly all the other lads had scattered, so there we were looking out for them. One of the specific instructions had been to stay out of the trees. So what did we see? Yes, Nigel Clough and Gary Crosby climbing up a tree – and they'd climbed to quite a height, waiting for the County lads to come with their ambush assault.

When we heard the whistle for battle to commence

Pearcey turned to me and said: "You know what, I'd love to shoot young Cloughie out of that tree." And just as he said that, we heard a scream and a crack as branches snapped and Nigel hurtled to the ground. He was screaming out in pain after hurting his ankle. We all ran over to check him out, but really we were laughing our heads off because it was so funny.

"My ankle's gone," yelped Nigel. We stretchered him off and promptly nicked his ammunition so we could get on with the game. We had a great time and thought no more about it. But the following day when we got to the ground, Nigel's ankle was up like a balloon. We had a big game coming up and he was going to be a big doubt. We pleaded with Nigel: "You've got to play because if you don't we're going to get shot by your old man."

To his credit, Nigel did his best to try to hide the injury. But there was no getting away from it and Cloughie went apeshit. "Who organised this paintball game?" he asked the lads as he hunted me down. "Ernie done it," replied my "mate" Pearcey. "It was nothing to do with me – he, that one there, he organised it." I tried to protest my innocence. "Gaffer, I didn't tell them to climb 20 or 30 foot up a tree," I said. "You bloody idiot," raged Cloughie. "That's our centre forward you've just nobbled. He's out injured now, so what are you going to do about it?" Cloughie was so angry I thought he was going to drop me for it.

Now here's what really happened. Nigel, if you want to know the truth, it was Stuart Pearce who shot you, not me! For all that, Psycho was a great player to have alongside you. I have never seen so many people have so much respect for one player. He was not technically brilliant but he didn't need to be. Stuart was just a totally full-hearted player who tackled so hard, always loved to get forward and had a murderous left-foot shot on him. He had a great rapport with the fans and would always wind them up to get behind us. It was the sort of bonding I have never seen before or since.

Luckily, I also got on well with the supporters. They liked a player who would give 100% and that's something I always did, even if I could never reach the same level of affection with them as Pearcey. He also had an unbelievable wit – but he needed it, too, because he had the worst taste in music I've ever known. Once, when I was in his car, I had the "music" of the Sex Pistols blasting out in my ears. I never wanted another lift from Psycho after that. That said, we had some great music nights out as a squad, seeing the likes of Mick Hucknall and Elton John.

Elton was a big admirer of Cloughie and would even be invited into our dressing room before games. Once he came in and told Cloughie he had some tickets for a concert he was doing at the NEC in Birmingham. Cloughie said he wasn't interested – but we would be. So off we went on the team coach with our wives and girlfriends, armed with these VIP tickets to meet Elton backstage just before he went on to perform. Just imagine if we had prepared for a big game by having a load of people in to see us! When the curtain went up, wow, Elton was brilliant. Actually, we did the same thing with Mick Hucknall who is a big Manchester United fan. We drank his courtesy bar so dry there was nothing left for him when he came off stage. And we also went as a squad to see Madness – which is quite appropriate when you think about who we worked for.

They say that madness and genius are so closely aligned they are almost one and the same thing. How else can you explain Cloughie picking a 19-year-old on the basis of watching him for just 45 minutes the day before? And he chucked him in for a debut against Liverpool at Anfield. Now that's what you call madness. But the player's name was Roy Keane. And that turned out to be pure genius. Nothing, I should add, to do with him being a Guinness-swilling young Irishman.

Even today it beggars belief how Keane came to make his debut. Cloughie had seen him for just 45 minutes in a reserve match. But what he saw was a boy playing like a man. So Cloughie plonked him on our team bus bound for Merseyside and we shared the journey with this scrawny, scruffy-looking kid who sat near the front and never said boo to a goose. Then again, not one player spoke to him. We just thought he was another of the young lads at the club who had been brought along for the ride. At Anfield he dutifully helped get the skips off the coach and into the dressing room. Cloughie then told him to start laying the kit out. When he got to the number 7 shirt, the gaffer said to Roy: "Go on, let's see what you look like in that."

The young lad look embarrassed as he put on the shirt. "Does it feel good?" asked Cloughie. "Good, then it's yours. Keep it on, you're playing." We all started to laugh, thinking it was a joke at the kid's expense. "He's PLAYING," declared Cloughie. "And you Lawsy will look after him. He's playing in front of you on the right hand side of midfield."

I thought: "Terrific." Not. I was even more shocked than the lad himself. Here we were at Liverpool, they were the league champions, they had got England winger John Barnes playing for them and he was on fire, and I'd got to babysit this young lad whose name I did not know.

Seriously, I didn't know a thing about him. And this was an hour before the game.

So I went up to him to introduce myself and he told me his name was Roy Keane. I promised to help him all I could and talk to him throughout the game. I explained the system we played but I feared all that would go out the window when we trotted on to the pitch. Barnesy could well have a field day. In fact, it was me who would be left looking the mug. Among other things, I'd pointed out there were times when I might need his help and that we would have to double up on Barnes. I told the lad where to be and what to do if I went tight with the England star. He was clearly keen to learn and seemed to take everything in. There was no fear in his eyes. And within five minutes of the game starting, all my doubts and fears were gone. Wow.

This kid had an engine on him like I'd never seen before, he tackled ferociously and he didn't give a shit for anybody on that park. And this was Anfield, by the way. Reputations counted for nothing with him. He kicked everything that moved – and in particular John Barnes. Once when Barnesy had been dumped on the floor he looked back up at young Roy and said: "Who the fuck do you think you are?" Roy Keane just stared him straight back in the face and told him to "fuck off!"

At that moment I knew the kid had more than a chance because he was already showing he could stand up to anybody. At 19, he did his job, did my job and everyone else's. What a find. What a capture. And what a stroke of genius by Cloughie. Now I knew why he had picked young Roy. He had seen enough in that 45-minute run-out for the reserves the previous day to convince him that this was a real star of the future.

The lad had been brought over from Ireland where he played for Cobh Ramblers. The princely sum of about £10,000 was the cost of his services. Roy quickly won his place in the centre of midfield, where he would spend the rest of his illustrious career, and he just ran the show for us. He was Keane by name and keen by nature, always getting up and down that pitch, sticking his foot in and being so aware of what was going on around him. I could see from those first moments at Anfield that he was a born winner. People get turned off these days when they hear about players earning £100,000 a week. Well, I'll tell you this – I would pay Roy Keane that. His managers knew what they were going to get from him before he kicked a ball. He was an absolute leader for any team he played for, an inspirational figure.

Yes, he's aggressive with it, but I think you have to have that in your nature if you are going to succeed at the top level. You need a will to win and a determination to take no prisoners if necessary. Even in his later years at Manchester United, after all his success (seven league titles, four FA Cups and the Champions League), he still had that same hunger burning inside him that I witnessed when he was a teenager. No wonder Sir Alex Ferguson built his team around him.

Roy had done some boxing in his formative years and it showed. He would fight his way out of a situation. Even as a youngster at Forest, he wouldn't be afraid to give a bollocking to a senior player. Some of them didn't like it, but he could stand up to them physically. Roy was someone who would never get bullied. On the other hand, he also had this huge smile and he simply loved playing.

There were times when Roy's antics on the pitch riled Cloughie. I remember he tried to do this roll-over somersault after a goal at Norwich one time. For one thing, it wasn't well executed and looked pathetic. For another, it incurred so much wrath from Cloughie that I'll be surprised if it's not still ringing in Roy's ears. Cloughie didn't like that sort of thing from anyone, let alone a young player. His way was to play smart and look smart, above all to be respectful. The manager would tell us never to rub it in the opposition's faces. There was no piling on top of each other to celebrate a goal, no jumping on to people's backs. Roy was told that if he ever did it again it would be the last game he played. Tough, but that was Cloughie's way of fathering him.

Not that Roy could be cowed. Remembering how he came to be sent home from the 2002 World Cup with Ireland, you won't be surprised to learn that he wouldn't accept sub-standard training even in his junior years at Forest. If it was a naff session he would say it was naff. He'd play hard, too, mind you. I remember him being sent home from a club tour of Jersey when Roy had had a few beers and things got out of hand. Cloughie was sitting in the hotel foyer waiting for him. He sent Roy packing, saying he was not prepared to take that from a young player. And Cloughie wouldn't be averse to giving him a clip round the ear to teach him a lesson. Otherwise, he could have had a real wild man on his hands.

I've stayed in touch with Roy and he helped me out when he was in his first management job at Sunderland and I was in a relegation fight at Sheffield Wednesday. Roy let me have an experienced midfielder called Graham Kavanagh. More than that, he arranged for Sunderland to subsidise Kavanagh's wages which were way above what we could afford. Sure enough, Graham helped us stay up. Besides being a good player, he was the sort who commands respect in the dressing room. Players can switch off at times. In an ideal world, you want the players to police themselves. When the control comes from their peers it can have more impact.

Another spin-off from knowing the young Roy Keane was the lesson learned from Cloughie about how to introduce young players to the first team. In particular, about how not to tell them until as late as possible. I never tell them two or three days in advance. That only causes worry and sleepless nights. It's a monumental occasion for any player. Another thing I do is always make sure their parents know, confide in them and make sure they are in the crowd for their son's big day. Cloughie made sure that Roy's parents were there at Anfield to watch him on that magical day.

10

Cloughie: The Passed Master

You can say his powers were waning or blame his habits. But the often overlooked element in the eventual downfall of Brian Clough was a simple change in the laws of the game. Simple but radical. And, considering Cloughie was such a progressive and pioneering manager, it's ironic that this was a rule designed to make football faster and more exciting. The game's lawmakers got in a huddle after some over-defensive play marred the 1990 World Cup in Italy. They came up with the back-pass law, introduced in 1992 whereby a goalkeeper could not pick up a ball played back to him by a defender. It could only be kicked by the keeper, cutting out what had been a natural break in the flow of the game. And that, as much as anything, was what killed Cloughie.

His decline could not be directly linked to the shattering of his FA Cup dream in 1991, much as his behaviour on that day was a sign of him becoming increasingly eccentric. We were back at Wembley twice more in the next 12 months. The final of the extravagantly-named Zenith Data Systems Cup saw us beat Southampton. Then we again reached the final of the League Cup, the competition we dominated in that era, only to lose to Manchester United. It was United's second successive appearance in the final, having suffered a shock defeat to Sheffield Wednesday a year earlier. This time they made no mistake, beating us 1-0.

It was now that the first cracks were starting to appear in the Forest success story. We finished a respectable eighth in the league in both 1991 and '92, but season '92-93 – the first of the new Premier League – saw us tumble from the top flight. Many pundits kept saying Forest were too good to be relegated. They were wrong. After the euphoria of beating Liverpool 1-0 in front of the Sky TV cameras in our opening game of the season, we went 10 games before our next victory. By then we were struggling near the bottom and this time Cloughie could not work his magic.

In many ways it would not be too harsh to say he had lost the plot, lost the grip he had on the team. I think he also lost just a bit of respect within the dressing room. The "I'll die for Brian Clough" cause was not quite there. He certainly liked a drink by this stage and it appeared to be getting the better of him. You wanted to say something to him but obviously you just couldn't. I would have loved to be able to say: "Come on gaffer, cut out the drinking and get a grip." In fact, all of us would like to have said something like that, but we were all too fearful.

Instead, one or two lunatic things started to occur. There are two incidents that I remember vividly. The first was when we played Tottenham on a bitterly cold, wet and windy afternoon. Despite the weather, Cloughie had a bee in his bonnet that he didn't want to sit inside the dug-out. So he got a wooden chair, placed it outside the dug-out and just sat there poker-faced staring down the pitch. Never once did he move. He just sat there like a statue in the pouring rain.

When Cloughie came in the dressing room at half-time he was shaking from the cold and the wet. He was trembling so much he couldn't speak to us. Instead, he simply sat in the corner while we got on with our own little jobs preparing for the second half. Not a single word came from Cloughie and it horrified me to see him like that. I thought: Is he going to keel over? Certainly, he looked awful. Forgive the irony, but he looked in dire need of a stiff drink there and then.

On the other side of the coin, Cloughie could be so funny in the amusing sense. After another game we played that season he was sitting there in the dressing room looking a little red-faced. I was drinking some cold water when he asked: "Is that nice?" I told him it was. "Right," he said. "I want you to pour a cup of water over my head."

I looked round at the other lads thinking it was a wind-up. "Are you sure?" I replied. "YES," insisted Cloughie. So I poured this cup of cold water over his head. It went down his face, his back, everywhere. I was still not sure what reaction I would get and was half expecting a bollocking. "That's perfect, that's beautiful," shouted Cloughie. "DO IT AGAIN!"

At that moment I felt like a child doing silly things with his dad. So I poured another cup of water over Cloughie's head. "Now throw it over my face," he demanded. So I poured another cup and really let rip. The water splattered all over his face – and he loved it. All the lads held their breath, wondering just what was going on. And we were all left open-mouthed as Cloughie simply said "thankyou", got up and walked away. By then there were a lot of things he did that left us confused. He would change the team on a whim and drop you for odd reasons. Things he said made you realise it was not the Brian Clough of old. In fact, he was just a shadow of his former self.

Along with this came the back-pass law. Without a doubt, that was the start of our demise at Forest. Nothing else really changed because we did the same pre-season that we had done for many years. Although it was always never enough for me, we could slow the game down under the old rules by passing back to the goalkeeper for him to pick up. This enabled us, with our style of play, to take a breather and play at a pace that suited our passing game. We had Des Walker, the quickest defender in the league, and he would win any ball played over the top before simply knocking it back to the keeper. That would kill any momentum built up by the opposition stone dead.

The new rule was only a small change but it was to prove so crucial for us. The pace of the game went from warm and tepid to scorching hot. If the powers that be wanted more action, they certainly got their wish. You can't knock the law change in any way because it resulted in more drama and, above all, more goals.

But it was clear that everyone in the game would have to adapt to it. Teams all over the country knew that fitness standards would have to be lifted. And to achieve that they were going to have to work harder. But we didn't do that at Forest. We tried to retain the style that had been so successful for us for so long. Almost inevitably, that was a major mistake. We continued to play well in games for 70 or even 75 minutes, but then we would run out of steam. The opposition would catch us out late on because their players were fitter and stronger. That's when we were weak, made errors and conceded goals.

As the season progressed, we all said to each other that we were not fit enough. Even players who had been at the City Ground longer than me and were more ingrained in the manager's methods recognised that we needed to do more work in training. But Cloughie simply wouldn't allow it, that was not his way. He would chase us off the training ground. It wasn't that we had to change our whole style. We could still play the way Cloughie wanted; but to do it successfully we had to be fitter. Unfortunately, there was nobody at the club who was strong enough to tell him that.

Halfway through the season, though, I think Cloughie did finally recognise the problem. Further, he allowed the coaching staff to try to do something about it. Ronnie Fenton was given the go-ahead to arrange for two fitness guys to come to the club. They took us training and various circuit programmes were set up. There was a weights circuit and a running circuit. No-one complained; we were all quite willing to do the extra work because we knew how badly it was needed.

We had been going for about an hour in the first session when Cloughie came along to have a look. Unfortunately, it had to be during a weights circuit. Cloughie saw us heaving these big weights and went spare. "What's going on here?" he roared at the instructors. "These are footballers, not weightlifters. What a load of bollocks this is. GET OUT!" And he got rid of them, just like that.

Eventually Cloughie did allow the fitness guys back. But they had to adjust their methods and water down their programme. By then, it was too late for us. Besides, there had also been rumours in the media about Cloughie's health and we could see for ourselves on a daily basis what he was like.

The end was hastened when one of the club's former directors hit out strongly at him in the press. He said Cloughie was drinking too much and had lost control. This kind of attack could only have come from outside the club. Certainly, the players felt far too much loyalty towards him to raise any dissenting voices. Cloughie had already talked about retiring, but this article pushed him to make it public earlier than he had wanted. Whether he should have gone straightaway, I don't know. But he stayed to try to keep the club in the Premier League, backed by a wave of emotion and goodwill that extended far outside Nottingham.

It pains me to say Cloughie was just a shell by this time. The spark had gone and he was very quiet in the dressing room. Towards the end we were effectively managing ourselves. This was not the Cloughie I had known and loved. Relegation was confirmed in a home defeat to Sheffield United on May 1st, 1993. The pictures of Cloughie told their own sad story. But he held his head high and was dignified to the last. Forest fans gave him the respect he deserved and the visiting Blades supporters chanted his name.

All the same, this was an awful, very unfitting way to end such a truly fantastic managerial career. But it would be wrong to dwell on that. Two generations of players across more than 20 years owed so much to this man. Without his foresight, intuition, inspiration and genius we would never have earned such a good living from the game or amassed so many treasured memories. I count myself truly lucky to have been signed by Brian Clough.

It was an even sadder day when he died in 2004. I don't know what the dress code is up there – but I'm sure they'll have made an exception for the man in a green jersey!

11

Colly-wobbles Along the Road to Management

One final scene with Cloughie was his attempt to block me taking FA coaching courses in preparation for a potential new career in management. But this was still a little way ahead and my last couple of seasons at Forest gave me a glimpse of one of the hazards of my new trade – handling difficult players. Stanley Collymore was a case study all on his own. But what a signing he proved to be for Frank Clark, who had returned to the City Ground from Leyton Orient to fill the great man's shoes.

Frank had played under Cloughie in the European glory days before taking charge of Leyton Orient and winning promotion with them. Forest needed a steady hand on the tiller and Frank's insight into the club's traditions was invaluable. But it looked a tall order for any manager when he arrived to take charge following our sorry relegation. It wasn't that the team wasn't good enough to come straight back, just that by the end of the summer there were very few of us left.

Cloughie's retirement spelled the break-up of his side. Roy Keane went to Manchester United for £3.75m, Nigel Clough joined Liverpool for £2.75m, Des Walker headed

Aged two with my sister Maureen – Simon Cowell look-a-like from an early age! What on earth was my mother thinking?

Burnside High School football team, seated front row, second left

Wallsend Boys Club players selected as Burnley apprentices. I'm at front right

A fresh-faced apprentice at Burnley FC in 1978

Pre season training with Martin Dobson, a true gent and great mentor

Goal scoring became quite a habit at Burnley. Not bad for a full back

In action at Turf Moor against Leeds United in August 1983
© Howard Talbott

Promotion celebrations, Burnley reaching the Second Division. I'm the one
wearing the jockey's hat!

Already barking orders in one of my first games for
Huddersfield Town

Away travel, and not an iPad in sight; a pack of cards was all
the entertainment we needed

In the garden with Danielle and Jamie shortly after signing for Middlesbrough

Why me? A streaker singles me out at Ayresome Park on a frosty night. Cover up man!

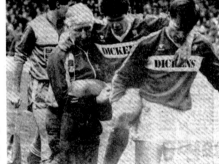

Desperate times. A cruciate ligament injury left me in rehab for a year

With Nigel Clough celebrating a
forest win at White Hart Lane

In action at The City
Ground, Nottingham

Great team spirit and camaraderie at Forest with Stuart Pearce
looking rather fetching in a wig!

Celebrations at Wembley, my first appearance of five as a Forest player

Forest V Luton, League Cup Winners 1989

Like it was yesterday.
Meeting Princess Diana
at Wembley

Daddy's little boy – son
Jaimie chosen as mascot,
Forest V Spurs

Cloughie never moved from the bench during extra time at the FA Cup Final.
His actions never ceased to surprise

We look on bewildered as the tragedy of Hillsborough unfolds before our eyes!
© Steve Ellis

A rare left footed goal for Grimsby

Italian Flair hits Grimsby – signing Ivano
Bonnetti in 1995

All is forgiven, at least in front of the cameras . . .
Chairman Bill Carr looking on, sorry Bill!

Time to celebrate. Scunthorpe United, League Two Play-Off Final winners 1999.
What a day!

Pride, the culmination of
hard work through the
season

Manager of the Year
Awards – season
1998-99

Promotion with Scunthorpe United, season 2004-05, dedicated to
chairman Steve Wharton, pictured with captain Andy Crosby

Introduction to the press accompanied by then
Sheffield Wednesday chairman Dave Allen
© Steve Ellis

Congratulations to Sheffield
Wednesday captain Richard Wood
© Steve Ellis

'Steel City Double', the owls victorious for the first time in 95 years. My great assistant, Russ Wilcox, and I celebrate with Kevin Blackwell looking on
© Steve Ellis

Directing from the Hillsborough touchline
© Steve Ellis

Five days old. Introducing baby son Thomas to 30,000 Wednesday fans in May 2009
© Steve Ellis

My local heroes, Daniel Grice and James Neal. Inspirational young men who are sadly missed having lost their fight against leukaemia

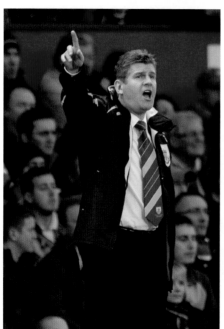

Welcome to the Premier League! A nice easy start as Burnley manager away at Old Trafford, January 2010
© Getty Images

On the touchline at Turf Moor, April 2010
© Getty Images

A proud day, marrying my beautiful wife Jane
in June 2004 by Lake Windermere

Mum and Dad at church

Party house – celebrating my 50th birthday with family and friends, October 2011

Sibling Support – big brother John and sister Maureen

Loving family – with Jane and my gorgeous children Danielle, Jaimie and Thomas, daughter-in-law Bo and grandson Kai

With Jane and Thomas on a relaxing holiday in Portugal, June 2012

for Sampdoria in Italy in exchange for £1.5m and Teddy Sheringham sealed a £2m switch to Spurs. Filling the Cloughie void was huge enough for any manager, just based on his name alone even if his powers had waned. Now there was a chasm in the dressing room. Despite all this, I signed a new three-year contract and trusted that some of the lessons that caught us out in the Premier League would be heeded. Frank ensured that they were. We became fitter and bonded again as a group. Apart from Collymore, that is. We were 10 players plus one in those days. But the success we enjoyed was worth the compromise. Here's how it all panned out.

Frank Clark made a smart opening move. He brought in every player at the club and asked them all individually why we thought Forest had been relegated. I know there was a lot said, a lot of steam let off. And I think Frank must have been shocked to hear the depth of feeling, especially about the fitness side of things. But I feel it also made him believe he had to do something very quickly to turn things around. That something, that bit of magic, turned out to be the signing of Collymore from Southend United. Doesn't sound much, does it? The signature of a striker from a backwater club? Yet Collymore, at 22, was THE big summer capture, joining others like my old team-mate Colin Cooper from Middlesbrough.

Cloughie had been looking at young Collymore, whose goals kept Southend above their station in the second tier, but refused to pay the asking price. It was enormous by the standards of the time – £2m. Considering there were add-ons rising to £2.75m, it was as much as Liverpool paid for Nigel Clough and more than Sheringham cost Tottenham. No wonder Cloughie shied away. But Frank's gamble –

financed by the departure of so many big names – paid off. Then again, while we bought into him, he didn't buy into us.

First, Clark laid down the sort of tough pre-season schedule that we should have been doing earlier. He recognised the shortfall and worked us damned hard. We also began to get some proper coaching on the training ground about the positional changes we needed to make to cope with the new back-pass law. One thing we had no need to change was our pride in having a great team spirit, the togetherness that counted for so much in the great years under Cloughie. But "Stan the Man" would never sign up for this. From the very first day in training it was clear that he was a loner. He was hard work to get along with. But I, for one, didn't mind grabbing on to his shirt tails if it meant getting some success. I didn't really care whether he fitted in or not providing he was doing the business out there on the pitch. And he did. That first year we went straight back to the Premiership as runners-up behind champions Crystal Palace. Stan proved himself as a big, strong and quick centre forward, a great player to work with on the field. He had everything. You would give him the ball, then just sit back and watch him. Often, he would go on and beat three or four players before putting the ball in the net. At times he could be awesome.

Now the downside. With all the accolades in the press, Stan started to believe his own publicity. He got a new contract at Forest – and he changed. Our first season back in the Premier League was a very difficult one when it came to bonding in the dressing room, particularly because of Stan. The club had appointed a fitness coach to work with us each day on specific warm-up routines. It was arduous work but I have always enjoyed that, preferring to be at the front of the pack rather than the back. There was this one occasion when we were running round the pitch at the City Ground – and Stan slowed down to a walk after just two laps! He wanted to do his own thing while we were left to slog through another eight laps or so.

I asked our fitness trainer if he was going to pull Stan into line. "Nothing to do with me," he said. "You just keep running." It was not the response I expected. So when I got round alongside the dawdling Collymore I took matters into my own hands. "Stan, come on – get back in it again," I said. He set off but soon started walking again and then just stopped altogether. He wasn't injured and this incident showed up his willingness NOT to work while everyone else was grafting away. I couldn't believe that the coaching staff seemed quite happy to let him get away with it.

When I tried to argue the point I was told to stay out of it, that it was nothing to do with me. But it was. As a player in the same team, I was determined to make it my business. So I followed Stan into the dressing room to make my point. "Stan," I said. "I like you. And I'm telling you something as a friend. You want me to bust my neck for you and win the ball for you in a tackle? And you're not willing to do this? I don't think so. Think again. This is a team game and you should be doing your bit with us now."

Stan's reply was typical. "Lawsy, you know what it's like," he said. "Mentally, I just can't get my head round this. I hate this long running."

I told him: "Fuck off, just get out there and DO it. It's not hard work, you can piss that, you know you can. You will be as strong as anybody out there. But I'll tell you this: If you don't then your team-mates are going to turn on you. They might not be saying anything now, but I will. I'm telling you now – but I WON'T tell you again!"

You could sense the feelings within the club towards Stan. But there was this great big dilemma. If we were to be successful again then we needed him. He said he would try to knuckle down. In fairness, he did give it a bit of a go for two or three weeks – before drifting back to his old ways again. If he switched off from us, we started switching off from him. Whenever he scored a goal for Forest all the other players would turn away. They didn't want to celebrate with Stan. That was their way of showing what they thought of him. He became an outcast in his own club because he couldn't demonstrate the commitment that was needed. It was sad, even more so in that Stan never learned his lesson. He had big moves to clubs like Liverpool and Aston Villa but remained a solitary figure before retiring at just 30. What a talent, but in many ways what a waste.

I was just coming up to my 33rd birthday in the season that started with Forest back in the top flight. Although I had signed a new three-year contract after Frank Clark was appointed, there was no guarantee of a place. Actually, that is true for any player but my age was beginning to count against me and it did make me wonder when Frank paid £375,000 to bring in Des Lyttle, another right back, from Swansea. I didn't want to leave Forest but knew the time was coming when I had to have a little look elsewhere.

My mind went back to the day I told Cloughie that I wanted to take the FA coaching badge. He went berserk! Cloughie had this bee in his bonnet about the FA. It had been buzzing around like mad since the time a few years earlier when he had been in the running for the England job. Cloughie really fancied it but the FA just wouldn't give it to him, even though he was the best manager out there at the time. He was too outspoken for them and claimed in turn that they did not have the "bottle" to give him his chance.

Nobody at Forest had any great coaching qualifications around the time I started to consider my long-term future. I'd had a serious knee injury which might limit the length of my playing career. Besides, I really fancied staying in the game. To do that, I needed to qualify as a coach and for that to happen I required the permission of the club. So I plucked up the courage to see the gaffer about the FA course.

"What the hell do you think you're doing?" growled Cloughie. "They know nothing. What are they going to teach you that I can't? You're not going to learn anything off them. English FA, what a load of rubbish. They can't even take a risk. They don't know what they're doing. In fact, I'll tell you what you *should* be doing – you should be going on holiday with me! I'll take you and your family if you drop this coaching nonsense!"

From anybody else, you might have taken such a bizarre offer as a joke. But Cloughie was serious and so was I. Coaching was something I had set my heart on and I was not to be tempted. Every time Cloughie tried to throw something at me to stop me going I would say flatly "no." I could see, of course, that he was getting irate and finally I turned round and said: "Alright, I won't take the coaching course if you'll guarantee me a job here at Forest when I've finished playing!"

Cloughie was fuming at that. "Smart arse," he said. But

he left it at that. He said no more and off I went to take the course that summer at Lilleshall. But there was a price to pay, you won't be surprised to learn. When I got back to the City Ground for the start of the next pre-season, Cloughie made my life hell from day one. He blasted off: "Oh my God, we've got an England coach in this camp now. What're we going to do, then?"

He would repeat himself every five minutes and it drove me barmy. But I tried to laugh it off, knowing he was upset. He'd let his feelings be known and now it was time to knuckle down again. But every time I made a mistake in training, he would rant: "Is that what you're going to teach your players? COACH? God help them, you know nowt. Is that what they teach you at the English FA? No wonder they're shite!"

This even happened in matches if I made a rick. Cloughie caned me. There was this game where we had a corner and I was back on the halfway line marking one of the opposition strikers. As he moved away I tried to follow him, but Cloughie bellowed: "Coach, stand still." And this was with the game going on around us. I was like a dummy. It was only when the the other team started to attack us that Cloughie finally let me move.

There was no sense or reason behind what he did, it was just Cloughie's way of making his point. But don't get me wrong. I was not the only one in that Forest dressing room who got the treatment. There were plenty of others. So, as you can imagine, there was hardly ever a dull moment. It was always quite enlightening. But it was also sad to see him going that way, almost falling apart in front of our eyes. Yet I don't think it was the pressures of management that got to him. He would never be affected by all of that.

Besides he was wealthy and had no financial issues.

Maybe it was something to do with his bust-up with his long-time sidekick Peter Taylor, who had been his right-hand man at Derby and in the early days at Forest. That cost him a close friend and he often told us he didn't have many of those. Whatever the reason, Cloughie seemed to lose his appetite, his desire and that vital spark with the players. We were like lost sheep and did not have our shepherd to guide us through a difficult period.

But the bottom line is that I loved Brian Clough. I had so much time and respect for him. He helped give me so many things in football that I had hardly dared to dream about. In my time at the City Ground I saw the best of Brian Clough and also the worst of him. I know what I'll remember most. And when I became a manager myself, it was only natural that something of him would rub off, however much I tried to be my own man.

The opportunity came much earlier than I expected. In 1994 I found out from a friend that there was a job coming up at Grimsby Town, then in the second tier. I was not yet ready to give up playing and here were Forest back in the Premier League, but I fancied management and decided to go across and watch a game at Blundell Park. I went through the motions of putting in a cv, which is standard practice for any would-be manager. But there were many much more experienced candidates to replace Alan Buckley who had left to take over at West Bromwich after doing an outstanding job with the Mariners.

Never in my wildest dreams did I expect to hear from Grimsby, let alone get a phone call from the chairman, Peter Furneaux, inviting me over for an interview. I was only too delighted to accept. Possibly they were attracted by the fact that I was playing for Nottingham Forest. Grimsby were a footballing side under Buckley and wanted to maintain that pattern – as I did, having been brought up in such a fashion. I think they were impressed with my thoughts at the interview. There was a common denominator between what they wanted and what I wanted. So I got asked back for a second interview with all the other directors.

This one lasted about two hours. After various questions were thrown at me, the directors thanked me and said they would be in touch. They knew I was still under contract at Forest but that Frank Clark was prepared to let me go if the right opportunity came along. Still, I returned to Nottingham with no real expectation of the matter being taken any further. Above all, I had absolutely no experience in management. For me, the exercise was more about building some knowledge about what to expect the next time I applied for a vacancy.

I have to say I was gobsmacked when the phone rang at home and it was Peter Furneaux. He wanted to talk to me again about becoming player-manager of Grimsby. I was really excited about that, but also nervous. But, once I was given the nod by the club's board, I was equally determined. I wanted to prove myself to a lot of people – maybe particularly to Cloughie. Perhaps I could say I was right all along about insisting on taking my FA coaching badge.

For the Grimsby supporters, my appointment must have been as big a surprise as it was to me. Although I carried a little bit of a "name", I think they were expecting an experienced bloke, certainly not a player-manager. All I asked of them, amid my trepidation, was to give me a bit of time and that I would have a good shot at it. Then they could judge me.

Where the board was concerned, I think they were a bit tired of being seen as a little club out in the sticks. They wanted someone who could give them a little more publicity. It was also important to them that I had a lot of contacts at a high level after my time at Forest. So, after six great seasons at the City Ground and 147 appearances for the club, I was heading for pastures new, swapping the banks of the River Trent for the Humber.

I climbed aboard the Mariners on December 1st, 1994, and I needed to learn my new trade as a manager very quickly. The first thing I found is that the transition is massive. Everyone thinks it's easy but let me assure you that is far from the case. And don't forget I was still a player, which makes it doubly difficult. Suddenly, instead of just thinking about yourself and preparing for each game, there are a hundred and one other things to do. You have to start thinking about 30 or 40-odd players, all with different characters and personalities, different weaknesses and strengths. And these are things you have to find out as quickly as possible.

Because of my lack of experience, the first thing I needed was to bring in someone to help. A lot of managers tend to bring in a pal, but I decided against that. Instead, I rang round people I knew in the game and the name that was recommended to me was Kenny Swain. He had been at Chelsea and Aston Villa as a player and then had a spell with Forest while I was there. Kenny had since been at Wigan as a manager and had knowledge of the lower leagues. That was going to be vital to me when it came to recruiting new players because the board had told me that effectively I had no money to spend.

Bringing in Kenny was purely a business decision. He was someone who had played under Cloughie, liked to play football, was not far from my own age and could be somebody I could lean on. I thought Kenny would be a good acquisition for me. In fact, he wasn't! I felt uncomfortable. I think he did a lot of groundwork around me that was unnecessary. I needed loyalty and 100% commitment from him. Unfortunately, I felt it wasn't there, I didn't get it. And this led me to do a naïve thing when a new chairman took over at Grimsby.

His name was Bill Carr and he turned out to be one of the nicest men I have ever met. Three times Bill asked me the question: "Do you feel you need to change your coaching staff?" Each time I said no – because Kenny had only just moved house from Cheshire to the Grimsby area and put his kids in school there. The right thing for me to have done would have been to say yes to the new chairman and to have changed my backroom staff. But a feeling of guilt would not let me do it. I suppose I didn't have the balls at the time to say I needed someone fresh to work alongside. I thought more about Kenny and his family than I did about myself and the decision I should have made.

I learned a very, very costly lesson from that. And I have learned it well because if the same situation ever happened again, I wouldn't have any fear whatsoever. I would replace instantly. I wouldn't even blink. I suppose it was all part of the learning curve for all new managers. They are going to make mistakes but it is only by making them and rectifying them that they learn the job. In a short period of time at Grimsby, I learned an awful lot.

That also tells you I made plenty of mistakes, but let me put another thing straight. I have never consciously tried to imitate anything that Brian Clough did. I have always tried to be myself. Equally, I am sure that after spending six years with him at Forest, something will inevitably have rubbed off. But I cannot pinpoint any incident where I have acted in the same way as Cloughie – unless you are talking about the Ivano Bonetti affair! Stand by your beds for that, it has a chapter all to itself and the truth will be told for the very first time. That bombshell was still some way from detonating when I rang Cloughie before I took the job at Blundell Park. His advice reinforces what I have just said. It was simply: "Be yourself. Always be yourself. It's a tough job, you'll find that. Trust no-one. But go and enjoy it."

Certainly, the role of player-manager made it especially tough and I would advise players coming to the end of their careers not to attempt it because it's just too hard. You are trying to justify your place in the team, so you are working just as hard as the rest of the players physically and actually trying to do better than them on the field because you are their manager. But when they leave after training, you stay. You can't switch off. You have to think about coaching, scouting, travel arrangements, preparing for games, writing your programme notes, talking to the different branches of the media.

After my first three months at Grimsby I was utterly and totally shattered. Believe it or not, I clocked up over 40,000 miles in that period going to watch every game that was available. I was trying to soak up every bit of information that I could, improve my knowledge of the players and teams we were facing in what was then called the First Division. Including reserve matches, I was averaging four games per week, also scouting out players who might become available to us. But a lot of it became pointless.

It got to the stage that whenever I stopped I slept, whatever time that was. I had this bee in my bonnet that if I was going to fail as a manager I would fail because of me, not because of relying on someone else. I wanted to do everything myself – the scouting, the coaching, everything. But it was killing my life. I knew I could not go on like that, something had to change. Realisation finally dawned. I would get to a night match at some far off place, gaze zombie-like at the pitch, wonder where on earth I was and then ask myself what the hell I was doing there anyway.

The penny dropped that you have to delegate and learn to trust other people. Trust is the biggest thing in football. Where I was fortunate was in inheriting a good squad of players from Alan Buckley at Blundell Park. Grimsby were established in the second tier despite having only limited resources and a small support base. They were always pulling rabbits out of the hat and that is a credit to the people associated with the club around that time. They were well organised and knew exactly what they were doing. It meant they always seemed able to perform above their means.

When I first arrived, I felt one or two changes were needed to take Grimsby another step forward. I wanted to put my own stamp on the team. I know that some "feeling" developed between Buckley and myself, although there had been no problems between us at the start. The friction involved Alan's son Adam, who had been left behind as a player at Grimsby when his dad left for West Brom. I rang Alan to ask him if he wanted us to cancel Adam's contract so the lad could join him at the Hawthorns. But he said: "No, the kid thinks he could get in your team and so do I."

This was awkward because, to be honest, I did not feel that Adam was really good enough and I suggested that it would be better if his dad took him. "No, give the lad a chance," Alan insisted. So I agreed, I had no real problems with that. But as time went on without Adam getting into the team, it got to the point where his dad rang me to say: "The lad's not happy and he wants to leave – but pay him up first."

That was something I was not prepared to do and it was the start of a spat. I reminded Alan: "I offered you the chance to take your son for nothing and you wouldn't. If you want him, take him. But what's he done to deserve us paying him up?"

Alan was not happy. "That's a disgrace," he claimed. I hit back: "Why? The lad has not played in the first team. Is it just because you're his father and you left him behind that you think we should pay him up?"

This was where Alan really snapped. "I'll get you for this," he stormed and slammed the phone down. He even contacted the board at Grimsby to try to get a pay-off for his son, but the directors backed my stance. What Alan should have known better than anyone was that Grimsby Town was, by First Division standards, a small club operating on a tight budget. If the truth be known, that's one of the main reasons why he had left and earned himself a fortune. But this was not about me or Alan, it was about Grimsby and we could not afford a pay-off for Adam. There was nothing personal, it was simply a sound business decision. But Alan still wasn't happy and ever since then it's really been a case of niggle, niggle, niggle between us. I felt he, as an experienced manager, was trying to get one over on someone who was still a novice in the job. So I became stubborn.

I don't know, maybe I handled it wrongly. But this kind of thing will always be part of football. It's a tough game and it hurts a lot of people. You don't get a lot of really close friendships developing within it. It's a cut-throat world among managers. We are all in the same job, trying to achieve the same things but naturally we are trying to outdo each other and the pressures are intense. You have to be strong-willed. Alan Buckley showed the strength of his will and I've had to learn to be the same. Alan didn't have any qualms about coming back to Grimsby and trying to take the best players with him to West Brom as cheaply as possible. That stuck in a lot of Grimsby people's throats. The one I particularly didn't want to see leave was Paul Groves. He was a good leader, which was what we needed, but we lost him.

Some changes were needed and it was against this background that I had a chance meeting with an agent I knew from my days at Forest. We bumped into each other when I was out scouting at Aston Villa one night and got talking over a cup of tea at half-time. He asked me what I was looking for and I said that one of my top priorities was a left winger. He told me he'd got one who was looking for a club. I asked him who.

"His name is Ivano Bonetti."

12

Bonetti and Me: The Truth at Last

For older readers the surname Bonetti will conjure up a former Chelsea and England goalkeeper. Yes, Peter Bonetti who, briefly and somewhat unfairly, became public enemy number one after he deputised for the sick Gordon Banks and became the fall guy for England's 1970 World Cup exit to West Germany. Well, in 1996, Ivano Bonetti was also at the centre of a national stir. Except that he wasn't painted as the villain of the piece. I was!

This was a controversy on such a scale that anyone over the age of about 36 must surely remember something about it. Or maybe you are younger and have heard about it from your dad. For most of the intervening years I have wanted this particular incident to be forgotten, to be brushed under the carpet. Now I rake it up again here for a simple reason – it's my chance to tell the real truth for the very first time. And let me tell you that this is one time when the facts of the matter are much more powerful than the fiction. A highly imaginative version of events has been passed down in folklore. I was the barbarian boss who flung a tray of chicken wings at one of his own players and put him in hospital requiring surgery for a fractured cheekbone. Actually it was worse than that. I THUMPED HIM! I caught him with my mean left hook!

But first you need to know the whys and wherefores: How I came to deck the Italian star who had put little Grimsby Town on the map even before the bust-up that created national headlines. And how I came to be plastered over the front pages as the devil incarnate. For that, we have to go right back to the start.

"His name is Ivano Bonetti," said my agent friend during that fateful scouting trip to Villa Park. "This boy is real pedigree. He has played in Italy in Serie A for clubs like Atalanta, Juventus, Sampdoria and Torino."

And so the sales patter continued: "He's over here in England now and looking for a trial." I was on the hook. After all, what did I have to lose? I said: "I will have a look at anybody of that quality – but does he know where Grimsby is? Does he realise it's a little fishing town on the east coast?"

The agent seemed to think the off-putting geography of the situation didn't seem to matter, even for a player used to the most exotic of surroundings. "Well, I think it does matter," I insisted. "Tell him it's near Manchester, that might help attract him!"

Actually I did know something of Bonetti. Once in a pre-season tournament at Forest I had played against him, me being a right back and him a left winger. I knew he had a bit of quality but he was now 31 – and what was he doing over in England? It was a climate and style of football that was hardly suited to him. Yet it seemed he was desperate. It transpired that he had been shopped around a number of clubs and that Grimsby was just about his last port of call. So I gave Bonetti an opportunity to play for the

Mariners reserves.

I announced this to the media once I had got international clearance for him. And for a game that would normally attract less than 100 punters, we had thousands turning up at Blundell Park. That incredible response alone told me that we might have hit on something here. If we offered him a contract there was the novelty value of an Italian playing in the Football League. Besides, his track record suggested pure quality. He had played for seven clubs in Italy . . . Brescia, Genoa, Juventus, Atalanta, Bologna, Sampdoria and Torino. Maybe I was a touch blinded by it all. Had I stopped to think, I might have asked why he had moved around so much, why he had stayed a relatively short time with each of them. On the other hand, you don't get to turn out for teams like those unless you can really play.

It seemed win-win all round. Grimsby would benefit on and off the field. Bonetti was sure to attract attention wherever he went. The only problem was, he wasn't fit. That was clear for everyone to see. But I sensed it was worth taking a chance with him and the board agreed. The next question was whether we could afford him. We had to come up with a package that would tempt him to the backwaters of Humberside. It was not easy dealing with Bonetti's negotiators, particularly as we had to use an interpreter. But one word stood out and it was new to us – "netto." Until then, the only thing I had heard called netto was a low budget supermarket! But it quickly became clear that it was all about lolly. Every figure we offered to Bonetti had to be "netto" – that is, after tax – rather than gross. We also had to arrange some accommodation and found him a log cabin at the Kenwick Park country hotel.

This cost the club £1,000 a month. We also got him a car and, of course, he always had to have an entourage of people around him.

This was real superstar stuff for a club like Grimsby. When Bonetti finally signed at the end of September, 1995, the town was buzzing. As expected, we put a lot more bums on seats. Bonetti quickly became a cult hero for the fans. They loved his extravagant style and, as an entertainer, he knew how to milk his audience. That didn't bother me at all – because the players responded to him, too, and we were winning games. If the playboy stuff was part of the process, all well and good.

The Bonetti factor snowballed to a degree where we were riding very high in the league and progressing in the FA Cup. In January, 1996, we were drawn at home to Luton Town in the third round of the competition and thrashed them 7-1. That wasn't far from matching the Mariners' record win in the competition, an 8-0 thrashing of Darlington way back in 1885. Our reward for hammering the Hatters was . . . a fourth round trip to the Hammers. It was in that tie with West Ham at Upton Park that the wheels started to come off the Bonetti bandwagon.

We had an injury at left back and I had to switch from the right to play there myself, behind Ivano. We opened really well, our confidence was high and the home fans were getting on the backs of the West Ham players. Then lo and behold, "Jinky Jim" on the left got hold of the ball, played a one-two with Steve Livingstone and steered a shot into the bottom corner to put us 1-0 up. No, it wasn't Bonetti. It was me! Fantastic, I was jumping around all over the place. But we knew there was more to come from West Ham who were bound to respond – and Ivano wasn't helping our cause. He kept giving the ball away and in the second half, when we were under real pressure, I needed him back to help me in defence. He wasn't always there.

West Ham equalised but we rode our luck and were hanging on for a replay. With about 10 minutes to go I made the kind of switch that any manager might have made in the circumstances. I shouted to Kenny Swain on the touchline to get Bonetti off and bring me on a defender from the bench. Ivano had these gloves on, as many foreign players seem to do in our winters, and he threw them in the dug-out as he walked past before heading straight to the dressing room.

No matter. We held out and when the final whistle went we were all elated. We had held the Hammers on their own ground and created the chance for the club to make more money while knowing that we could beat them in the replay back at our place. But there was a niggly little problem waiting for me in the dressing room. As I've explained, Ivano had an interpreter. He would be in the dressing room at our games and even on the bench during them. Now I don't understand Italian – well, not much anyway – and I have no idea what the interpreter used to tell Ivano when he translated our comments. Whatever it was, it often didn't seem to bring the response we expected. And so at Upton Park I was told that I had "embarrassed" Bonetti in front of his family by bringing him off.

I told the interpreter to tell Ivano not to be so daft. I had only substituted him for tactical reasons and he would be playing again in the next match. Frankly, I couldn't be bothered with the sulks of one player just because he had been brought off in what had been a terrific night for the club. Grimsby Town was bigger than Ivano Bonetti.

The next match, in advance of the Cup replay, was in the league away to the Luton side we had murdered 7-1 in the third round. And this was the game that many of you will have heard about. The date was February 10th, 1996. Once again I was playing at left back and by half-time all was going to plan. Jamie Forrester had put us into the lead and we were passing Luton off the park. Jamie then scored another. But from that seemingly unassailable position we fell apart. We had a centre back called Vance Warner on loan from Nottingham Forest and he had a nightmare second half. Luton scored twice from his mistakes and went on to beat us 3-2.

I was not happy. I was boiling. One of the things going through my mind as I walked off the pitch at Kenilworth Road was just what I was going to say to Vance. I was something like the third man back into the dressing room – where Luton had left the usual complimentary tray of food for the players. From memory, there were sandwiches, sausage rolls . . . and chicken legs.

As I walked through the door, Ivano was already standing over the food eating. Now for me, the last thing that should be on your mind when you have just walked off the pitch after losing a game you should have won by a mile is wanting to eat. Have a drink, yes. Eat, no. Other than that, I didn't have any real argument to pick with Ivano – my thoughts were solely concentrated on Vance. Physically, I was drained after a hard 90 minutes but mentally I wanted to have my say about what had gone wrong out there.

I ordered Ivano to forget the food and sit down. He looked back at me and muttered something in Italian. I couldn't understand the words but I knew from his body language that he wasn't happy. But then neither was I. "You can cut it out," I barked. "You're very clever when we're sitting talking about money because you can understand that. Well, I'm telling you now, sit your fucking arse down and let me do my team talk."

At this point Bonetti came in my direction. He was holding sandwiches and he threw them at me. Then he took a swing. He caught me on the chin. In that split second, with my emotions still burning after what had happened on the pitch, I did what I honestly feel a lot of people would have done if somebody had thrown the first punch. I threw a punch back. Just one punch. Not the tray with the chicken legs that was reported in the media at the time and has been mentioned ever since. It was a punch, pure and simple.

Down went Ivano. "That's you finished at this club," I shouted at him. In fact, I could easily have been shouting those words at myself! By this time, the club physio was tugging on my leg to pull me away and as I turned I said to the rest of the players: "I'm sorry you've seen that. But he was right out of order there."

In fact, I became glad they did see it – because they could all verify my version of events. At the time I thought I had just knocked Bonetti over, nothing more and nothing less. I wasn't aware of how hard I had hit him and there was certainly no intention to do him any harm. I was simply making a point in the most natural way considering the heated nature of the circumstances. I'm sure Cloughie in his prime would have done exactly the same. People always asked me if I learned anything from the great man – perhaps I did!

When the physio told me he thought Ivano might

have a broken cheekbone I was staggered. Suddenly the interpreter was there in front of my face screaming that they would sue me for what had happened. I told the physio to take Ivano to be checked out by the club doctor at Luton while I spoke to the rest of the players.

"What you have just seen stays in the dressing room," I insisted. "Remember everything you have just witnessed – but don't talk to anybody." Then I told them to get changed and back on to the team coach, while I went off to find out more about what was happening with Ivano. Apparently he was heading for a hospital in Luton to have an X-ray. I told Kenny Swain to go with him. Then I sent for the chairman, Bill Carr, to come down to the dressing room along with the other directors who had travelled. I told them there had been an incident and explained everything that had happened.

I didn't hold back. "At this moment I am still in shock, but if this gets out then it's going to be big," I said to the directors. And I offered to stand down. "If you want me to resign I will," I added. They could have got rid of me there and then. Instead they gave me their full backing. They accepted Bonetti had been in the wrong and were more than happy to stand by me. But this, of course, wasn't the end of the episode. How could it be?

The directors left me to get changed and I just sat there in the bath for about 10 minutes, staring straight ahead with everything still flashing through my mind. I knew full well that my split second of retaliation could have ruined my career. If the story leaked out, there would be mayhem. Fat chance, really, of keeping a lid on it. There are very few secrets in football.

On the journey back to Grimsby I asked the players to

write down exactly what they had seen. I was not asking them to tell lies to protect me, just to put down the truth as they saw it. Their accounts were then locked away in the safe back at the club. On that homeward journey the commercial manager, Tony Richardson, came and sat next to me. I told him I didn't know what to do. "Do nothing," he advised. "We will sort things out when we get back."

The coach dropped me off in Nottingham, where I was still living at the time, and as I got off I was physically and violently sick. I wasn't ill in the normal sense. This was shock and nerves. I was still in a daze when I got home and told my family what had happened. Kenny Swain, who was still at the hospital in Luton, rang to tell me Ivano was to have an operation the next day.

Predictably, my hopes of keeping things quiet were blown apart. Ivano's people were in touch with Sky television and they went down to see him at the hospital, finding him "battered and bruised." Once the TV cameras were on the scene, the national newspapers soon followed. The shit had hit the fan. I was in the headlines big style.

I was absolutely devastated to see the pictures of Ivano. From hardly having a mark on him, he looked as though he had done 10 rounds with Mike Tyson. And I can never forget the front page headline in the Sun which read: "COULD YOU WORK FOR A MAN WHO DOES THIS?"

I became a recluse. I didn't want to go out because of the embarrassment, not that I could do anyway. I had camera lenses popping through the conifers in my garden and was effectively imprisoned at home. There were cars parked outside all the time and it was very uncomfortable. You see these superstars who have paparazzi following them every day, knowing they can't sneeze without having a camera in their face. That is the norm now – but it wasn't then. If I've ever understood the life those modern day celebrities lead then that was the time.

After speaking to the club, they said they would issue a statement. When I finally got to the ground for the first time since the bust-up, the place was besieged by the media. I told reporters there was to be no comment pending the statement. I had already been advised by both the Football League and John Barnwell, the chief executive of the League Managers Association, to say nothing. And that's the hardest thing to do when you want to put your side of the story. But looking back, they were right. There are always two sides to a story and I wanted to present mine. The only side that was seen was the one put across by Bonetti and he milked it. So it was tough to keep quiet. But in the long-term the LMA and their lawyers were spot on. Had I said something, the story could have spiralled even more out of control. Besides, I didn't want a slanging match. I wanted to draw a line under things as quickly as possible.

During all that was written and said about me I had to bite my lip. I was being hounded at the club, hounded at my house and my son Jamie even got involved in playground scrapes because of what had happened. In the middle of everything that was going on around me, I decided to turn for advice in what might seem to be an unlikely direction. I rang Bruce Rioch, my old boss at Middlesbrough with whom I had fallen out during my departure from the club.

I knew Bruce had been involved in an unsavoury incident himself while he was in charge at Torquay and he had resigned over it. "Don't do anything," Bruce insisted. "Forget about it and just get on with your job."

Easier said than done, of course, but I received exactly the same advice from other senior managers I rang, including the old Bald Eagle himself Jim Smith. They all knew that much worse things have happened in a dressing room. I was just unlucky that this one had got out. Instead of isolating themselves from me, these fellow managers were all supportive and I really appreciated the messages that came from them.

Almost forgotten amid all this drama was the big game coming up at Blundell Park, the FA Cup fourth round replay with West Ham. Somehow, we had to clear the decks for that. I am sure the players were wondering all sorts of things. Was I still going to be there as manager or would I go? It was obvious what was going through their minds. I had that same feeling when I was at Forest and Cloughie smacked those two supporters who ran on the pitch. We doubted he would survive that but, of course, he did.

I went into the dressing room, sat the players down and spoke to them. "Look, you have just got to carry on playing," I said. "Everything else will sort itself out one way or another. Whether I am still here does not really matter. You have got a job to do. That is against West Ham and you've got everything to play for."

By this time I'd even had a phone call from Hammers boss Harry Redknapp offering his support. Not many managers in his position would have done that before an important cup tie. The Grimsby board met again, this time with Bonetti and his representatives, looking for a solution satisfactory to both parties. "Could we still work together again," they asked me. In truth, I didn't want to work with Bonetti after all that had happened. But for the sake of the football club I said "yes." Ivano made the same agreement and we prepared to put out a statement before the cup game.

Normally we would be lucky to get half a dozen press photographers at Blundell Park but on this night there must have been about 40 or 50 of them. The deal was to make a prepared statement out there on the pitch. Then I had to shake Ivano's hand. I did, but it was the worst handshake of my life. We barely looked at each other. It was just a show of unity for the sake of the public. This was what the fans wanted to see, but behind it there was nothing. Certainly, it meant nothing to me and I am sure Ivano felt exactly the same. It was just a public relations exercise.

Still it worked a treat and the supporters were cheering from all sides of the ground. The atmosphere that night was electric and the Grimsby players responded to it. They went on the rampage. West Ham couldn't handle it and we won 3-0. It was an awesome, awesome night of football. One almighty high after the greatest low of my career. The only downside was that I couldn't take part in it as a player. The previous few days had left me emotionally drained. Remember this was my first full season as a manager – a player-manager at that – and I was still striving to cope with the job.

The Bonetti controversy could have sunk me before I had learned to swim. But it didn't. After the game I went into the dressing room to thank each of the players in turn. They had been inspirational, showing me what they were made of and proving themselves a real pleasure to work with. I could feel myself welling up inside and had to leave the lads before my emotions kicked in. I went up to my office, closed the door and, for the first time, opened a bottle of whisky and took a big swig out of it. Then I bawled like a baby! I couldn't control myself. All the bottled up feelings just flooded out. Kenny Swain walked in and poured me another drink to calm me down.

Perhaps I had a chance to put the Bonetti saga behind me and the board continued to be supportive. But still it dragged on. By now the insurance people had become involved. The advice I was getting from everyone was that I must try to get Ivano fit again. In truth, I would have loved to have got rid of him there and then. I knew his continued presence at the club was going to make life difficult for me. He would be there in that dressing room and goodness knows what he would be saying and doing behind my back. His English was getting a lot better, too. Nevertheless, I had to get him fit and be careful how I did it. I had to make sure he knew exactly what instructions we were giving him.

There was to be another occasion when he tested my patience to the limit. It was raining and Ivano told me he could not train in rain. "It affects me!" he said. He'd only had a fractured cheekbone for Christ's sake. Didn't it ever rain in Italy? I knew he was simply trying his best to wind me up, so I had to back off. Bonetti had me exactly where he wanted. Every time he got an opportunity, there would be an article in the press. But still I could not respond. It was killing me. By nature I am someone who, when faced with a problem, wants to deal with it there and then. But this time my hands were tied. I could not do a thing.

Managers have to have discipline within a club but I could not enforce it with Ivano. If a player is late turning up for training, he gets fined. But if I acted against Bonetti he would say I was picking on him. I had to handle him with kid gloves. But even that wasn't the answer because I knew full well where all of this was going. All the signs were there. He was going to sue the club and he was going to take everything he could get.

Confirmation finally came through from the insurers that Ivano had started legal action for an industrial injury. Although the action was in fact against Grimsby Town, he thought it was being taken against me personally. He wanted my bank account frozen and reluctantly I had to agree, as this was all part of the plot. Eventually we got him fit enough to play a few games . . . before the blessed day arrived when I was able to release him at the end of the season when his contract was up. The biggest relief I have ever had in football was the day I saw the back of Ivano Bonetti.

I could not believe my eyes or my ears when John Aldridge, my old FA Cup semi-final adversary, took him to Tranmere Rovers. Aldo had previously asked for my opinion of Ivano and I told him: "As you can well imagine, I could be very, very biased. But I'll be honest. He can excite the crowd, one game in five he might be outstanding – but for me he's a shit!" I could have told Aldo a pack of lies but gave it to him straight. All the same, he signed Bonetti and he was welcome to him. I suppose it was a kind of poetic justice after the 1989 incident. The following summer I met Aldo while on holiday and he said: "I can't believe I took Bonetti. The players hate him, I hate him and I could not wait to get rid of him. He was a pain in the arse."

When Bonetti's legal action with Grimsby was finally settled it was out of court. He got £40,000 damages with £60,000 costs. And he went away happy. Some time later he even had the audacity to try to buy the club before switching his attentions to Dundee in Scotland. Things were never quite the same for me at Grimsby after that. Ivano might have been out of the way but his presence lingered. I feel the episode contributed to my eventual dismissal from the club. It caused me to lose a bit of faith from the supporters and, more importantly, the players seemed to lose direction. I am not saying Bonetti was the reason for me being sacked but he was certainly a factor.

We needed a good start to the following season but the results were not as good as anticipated and pressure started to build. I identified a particular player who I thought could help turn things round and planned to ask the chairman if we could buy him. But before I got the chance, Bill Carr came in to see me. I had got on so well with him during my time with the club. He had always been a big help, never more so than during the Bonetti crisis. I sensed that something was on his mind but never dreamt that my tenure was about to come to an end. Realisation only dawned as I saw that Bill could not look me straight in the face. He didn't say much, but he didn't have to. He found it hard telling me that I was being dismissed. This was the first time he had had to do anything like that.

"Bill, just do what you have to do," I told him. "You have to make your decisions. I won't take it as personal." And I never did. Bill and his wife Josie were a lovely couple. He would come over to watch games at Scunthorpe when I became manager there and I was much saddened when he passed away.

Looking back, I could not have wished for a better club than Grimsby to start my managerial career and I have a lot to thank them for. I made mistakes, probably a lot of mistakes, but I think I made some good decisions as well and, on balance, I feel I did well for them. My two years at Blundell Park were invaluable. I experienced things in that short time that managers who have been in the game for 20 years might not have had to cope with.

You can learn to curb your emotions but one thing you cannot change is the emotional nature of football. I would not be human if I did not blow my top at times because I want perfection and 100% endeavour from my players. I respect supporters and know how much they pay to watch their team on a Saturday afternoon. Out there on the pitch there is nowhere for a player to hide. If they don't give their all then the crowd will spot them. And if the fans spot them it's damn certain their manager will, too. All I ever ask is that players give their best – and if they do that, I will back them all the way.

Another positive to come from the Bonetti episode was the experience of handling a media frenzy. It was a crash course in public relations and has helped me deal with the sort of pressures that surround every manager. I came to understand that the journalists' interest in me was not personal. They were there to do a job. An acceptance of that is an important lesson when it comes to trying to make the best of a bad situation. You can feel like telling people to piss off. But this was a big story and I understood the attention focused on me. So I tried to deal with the media calmly and professionally. There are no courses to help you cope with such a situation. It could have turned really nasty, so I felt I handled it quite well. Otherwise, I could have been finished there and then. And if such a thing had happened today it probably would have finished me.

13

Tearing a Strip off Them at Scunthorpe

They say there is only one certainty about being a manager and that is getting the sack one day. Whether it is sooner or later, it will surely happen. For me, it was sooner. I'd only just started in the job and here I was out on my ear at the age of 36. But, looking back now, I'm quite proud to think I lasted two years in my first post. Hey, that's an eternity compared to the kind of tolerance given to first-timers these days. Some of them are lucky to last two months. And if you are seen to fail first time out, where do you go after that? Who will have you?

The key words are "seen to fail." It's a perception thing. Can anybody really fail after a few weeks and months?

Luckily, I managed to make a bit of an impact in my time at Grimsby – in more ways than one! Maybe I would have disappeared off the radar without all that publicity, good and bad. But it was still an empty feeling to find myself out of work. Looking back, perhaps it was a good thing that I experienced it at a comparatively early age – because the chances are that you will be on the shelf more than once.

I drove away from Grimsby back to Nottingham still in

a state of shock about what had happened to me. Getting sacked left me in a daze. The reality did not really sink in until I saw the news on teletext and later in the newspapers. Even then, it took me a couple of days to come round. I am sure all managers go through the same emotions after being dismissed. You feel very low and start to think of yourself as a failure. But there was no doubt in my mind that I still wanted to be a football manager. In fact, my resolve was strengthened. After so much had happened to me in such a short time, I felt it could be put to good use. And I think the overall experience toughened me up as a person. The hardest thing to deal with is that the telephone at home goes dead. Before that, it had been red hot, dealing with all sorts of people . . . directors, players, other managers, the media. Suddenly it's as if you no longer exist.

It's commonplace, of course, for managers between jobs to be in this vacuum state for months or even years. I suppose you could call it suspended inertia. Once you have recovered from the blow and had a short break, you are full of energy and ideas which have nowhere to go. Or at least that's what they tell me. I've been lucky enough not to have too much experience in that regard having worked fairly constantly right up until losing my job back at Burnley at the end of 2010. And by then, at 49, I was mature enough to appreciate a bit of time off with the family and to embrace it. After all, I'd never had an extended break since starting as a player. And it was because I was still young enough to play back in 1996 that I was soon involved in football again. That proved to be the ace up my sleeve.

When the phone finally rang the man on the other end was Gary Bannister, a former Sheffield Wednesday striker who was assistant manager at Darlington. Gary said he knew I could still play and asked me if I fancied joining the Quakers to take my mind off what had happened to me at Grimsby. I saw it as an ideal opportunity to start again. Feethams was well removed from Grimsby and this was a chance to recover my hunger for football. Although I had not been involved as a player during my latter days with the Mariners, I had still trained every day with the team, so my fitness levels were quite good.

But what a culture shock playing for Darlington proved to be. Remember that I had been accustomed to playing in the top two divisions and had represented one of the finest sides in the land during one period. I went up to play a match for Darlington and remember standing beforehand on what passed for a pitch. It was pouring with rain and it was a horrible playing surface. I thought: "What am I doing here?" I don't mean to be disrespectful to Darlington but that's just the way it was as I joined the club on a non-contract basis. Fortunately, it was not to be for long, much as I was grateful to Gary for bringing me back into the fold.

The second of my nine league games with the Quakers was against Scunthorpe United at Glanford Park, where we lost 3-2. The man in charge of Scunthorpe happened to be Mick Buxton, my old boss at Huddersfield. A little while later Mick contacted me and asked if I fancied joining the Iron. It was an easy decision. I was not enjoying my time at Darlington and Scunthorpe was much nearer to my home in Nottingham. So I told Mick I would sign for him – and it certainly wasn't for the money. It was just to keep playing and stay involved with football. At the same time, I made it clear to Mick and Scunthorpe that if a managerial vacancy cropped up then I would probably want to try for it.

Mick was quite happy with that scenario. Never did I expect that the first vacancy to arise would be at Glanford Park! And that I would end up filling it. But let me tell you there was nothing sinister about the events that unfolded. I had a lot of time for Mick, who had helped me as a young player. This was his second spell at Scunthorpe and he was having a hard time. The fans were starting to have a go and I felt for him. I am sure there will have been some people who believed I came to Glanford Park looking for Mick's job, but that was not the case. I was only interested in looking elsewhere. When Mick was sacked I did not apply for the job. I was asked.

There were talks with the then chairman Keith Wagstaff at which I said I would be interested and it just went from that point. We sat down and thrashed out a deal that would make me player-manager. Mark Lillis was to stay on as my assistant, as he had been under Mick. That was no problem for me as I had played with Mark at Huddersfield. We knew each other and had an immediate rapport.

It was my second job as a manager but the first time I had taken charge in the lower leagues. This was what they called the Third Division – in other words, the basement. Now throw in the fact that I was a football purist. Couldn't be any other way after six years with Cloughie. I have always wanted my teams to play football – and still do. But I quickly learned that lower down there are times when you can knock it around and times when you can't. There had to be a compromise in my principles and beliefs. But I still learned the hard way. I wanted to play attractive football and we did. Having brought in good players like Jamie Forrester and Justin Walker, we played some confident stuff. But it was still not enough to get us promotion.

During the middle part of my first season at the helm, we suffered an horrendous run. It stretched to eight successive league defeats, a club record. We were still playing entertainingly and were involved in the cup competitions, but we were simply falling short time after time in the league. And it all came to a head on a bitterly cold January evening at Macclesfield where we lost again 2-0. That was the night when I decided that, against all my beliefs, things had to change. Drastic action was required and I put my plan into force the very next day when we had a reserve game. I played all the first team in the reserves with orders to adopt a new style and a new philosophy. We had never had a big fellow up front, for a start. So I switched Mark Sertori from centre-half to lead the attack. He was a great professional and ran his socks off in an unfamiliar role. The other players were also given specific instructions on how to go about things.

Their response was instant and terrific. Starting with a home win against Swansea, we suddenly went on a good run that turned our season around. Despite those eight successive defeats either side of Christmas and New Year, we ended up only missing out on the play-offs by a single point. I still wanted my Scunthorpe team to play attractive football when possible, but I knew we also had to meet the physical demands of the bottom division. That's why I went out that summer and brought in big John Gayle, a rough and tough striker who had been part of Wimbledon's success story. John was my best signing for the sheer fact of his size and his presence on the field. His presence in the dressing room was also to prove important for us. John was the proverbial gentle giant off the field but he was simply a giant on it. He would run through brick walls for you and it was around him that a terrific team spirit formed. The players who benefited most from John were our other two strikers, John Eyre and Jamie Forrester, who grabbed 40 goals between them in our promotion season of 1998-99.

Right from the start of that campaign I knew we had a real chance. There were three automatic promotion positions and, of course, you set out by aiming for one of those. But if ever there is a preferred way to win promotion then there is nothing better than doing it through the play-offs and winning at Wembley. Yes, it prolongs your season and requires an extra effort but it also galvanizes the whole town and creates a powerful memory that carries over an impact into the following season. If we had gone up automatically it would have been all over in one afternoon in front of maybe 4,500 supporters at Glanford Park. Such occasions tend to be quickly forgotten. But the play-offs can be something special. Admittedly, they have the potential to be a source of frustration and if you keep missing out in them, they are something to be avoided. But the chance of going to Wembley was still a novelty for a club and a town like Scunthorpe. The Iron had been there just once before, losing a play-off final to Blackpool in a penalty shoot-out seven years earlier.

We drew the short straw in the semi-finals in being presented with a long journey to Swansea in the first leg. We knew it would be difficult at Vetch Field against a physical side in a partisan and intimidating atmosphere. I realised it was crucial to get my team selection right and came up with one or two surprises, bringing in Tim Clarke and Steve Housham. In fact, I went against the advice of my coaching staff in picking Tim as our goalkeeper in place of Tommy Evans. I just felt that Tim, at 6′ 4″, had the extra presence that was needed to counter the aggression I knew we would face in our box. Tim was not as agile as Tommy but I knew he would rise to the challenge of commanding his area. Tim was as surprised as anyone by my decision but I felt it was the right thing for that particular game. Horses for courses, if you like. It could have backfired. But it didn't and worked well for us.

Meanwhile, Steve Housham gave us the aggression we needed in midfield and nearly grabbed the bonus of a goal in that first leg. We came away with a 1-0 defeat which was a good result in the circumstances. I'd have probably settled for it beforehand because I was always confident we could reverse such a deficit back at Glanford Park in the second leg.

What an emotion-packed night it proved to be. The atmosphere was fantastic and the game had more than enough excitement in it for everybody. We got the early goal we needed to level the aggregate scores courtesy of a cracker from Andy Dawson. The teams stayed all square and the real drama unfolded in extra-time. It was then that the Scunthorpe fans found a new hero in the unlikely shape of a teenager called Gareth Sheldon who had come on as a substitute late in the second half. Gareth had only a handful of first-team games under his belt, but he took this big occasion by the scruff of the neck to make it a night of glory for us. Sheldon put us 2-1 up on aggregate early in the first period of extra-time. Suddenly those twin towers were looming in front of us – only for Swansea to grab a crucial away goal to level the overall score. Had it stayed that way, John Hollins' team would have been going to the final under the away goals rule. But young Sheldon came up trumps yet again with the goal that sealed our 3-2 triumph and put us through to a final against Leyton Orient.

It was a proud, proud moment for me to take Scunthorpe to Wembley where I had enjoyed so much success as a player with Forest. You can never beat actually playing, but being a manager is certainly the next best thing. This was my first real taste of success as a boss and it made me hungry for more. We prepared for the final with a short break in Ireland. This was to train for a couple of days but otherwise to relax and enjoy the great team spirit we had fostered.

The day before the game I took the squad to Wembley itself for a walk round the pitch and a look into the dressing rooms. They used to have a tape of crowd noise which could be played on the tannoy during group visits. This was used for us so that our lads could get a taste of match atmosphere as they walked around the pitch. And even though it's not real, it doesn't half make the hairs on the back of your neck stand up. I knew it was important to give the players an indication of what to expect. They might never get another chance to play at Wembley and this Friday visit to the stadium really helped us the following afternoon.

It was a great sight to see 12,500 Scunthorpe supporters at the game. That was a terrific effort for a town of our size . . . three times as many as if we'd won promotion by the automatic route. It must have been a ghost town back in Scunthorpe that day. Although our fans were outnumbered two-to-one by the Leyton Orient supporters from London, the noise they made was incredible.

I always felt this was a game we were going to win,

even when we were in the tunnel waiting to come out to the roar of the crowd. Before a ball was kicked, Big John Gayle was immense for us in the way he wound up the opposition. I remember him standing there bouncing the ball and then bouncing it off the head of one of the Orient players. A few of them swung round to say something to him, but when they clocked his size and saw the whites of his eyes they turned quickly away. I could sense from their reaction as we stood there in the tunnel that there was nothing to worry about.

It is now written in Scunthorpe folklore that Alex Calvo-Garcia headed the only goal of the game. This was scored after just seven minutes from a cross by young Gareth Sheldon. The kid was deputising for John Eyre who, heartbreakingly for him, was suspended after being sent off in the second leg against Swansea. Not that Alex's goal was by any means the end of the drama. After playing well in the first half, we made life difficult for ourselves by not adding to our lead. It was a nervous second half as Orient searched for an equaliser. But we were well served by our goalkeeper Tommy Evans, the man I had replaced with Tim Clarke in the semi-final at Swansea. I brought Tommy back at Wembley because his performances in the second half of the season deserved for him to be there. And he justified my faith in him with some fine saves. The final whistle seemed a long time coming but it was worth the wait. What a fantastic feeling, what a great way to go up. People in Scunthorpe still talk about it to this day.

If there was one downside for me, now a manager rather than a player, it was that the celebrations had to be short-lived. Players can savour such triumphs for weeks but managers have to get straight back down to work again, not least because the play-offs have already taken a bite out of your summer. After a gap of just two days we had to get down to talking contracts again with the players. The Bosman ruling had just come in and we knew that could create problems for us in that some of our players would become the focus of attention. But certain key players had previously told me they would be happy to stay if we were promoted. I believed them at the time and it disappointed me when their attitude suddenly changed. So soon after Wembley, their answer to the question was different. I had been kidded. When the contracts were put in front of them, their response was a quick "no." In hindsight, I had been naïve.

All I had asked from the players was honesty. If they had told me their true thoughts when we had spoken earlier I would have had the time to look for replacements. As it was, important players like John Eyre and Jamie Forrester walked out of the club for nothing – and I had just four weeks to fill the gaps before the start of pre-season training for life in a higher division. By this time all the best players had gone and we were left scrabbling around. It ended up meaning that we had a youngster in Wayne Graves partnering Gayley up front when we kicked off in the Second Division at Wigan Athletic's new JJB Stadium. I had to resort to looking at players on a trial basis and one of those was Guy Ipoua. What a find we thought we had there. Guy had been released that summer by Bristol Rovers and came to Glanford Park when his agent rang to ask if we'd fancy taking a look at him. Everywhere else he'd been for a trial he'd failed. But I was struggling and so short of numbers that I put Guy straight on the bench for a home game against Bournemouth.

We put Guy on at the start of the second half and he was terrific. He scored a goal in a 3-0 win that was a real spark for us. It was our first victory of the season and the fans took to Ipoua immediately. We gave him a contract until the end of the season, but after just three games he came knocking on my door saying that he was scoring goals and wanted more money. Such is the way the game has gone and such is the lot of the modern manager. It was the start of a "love affair" between Guy and me. For all his early impact, he was the worst trainer I'd ever had. He spoiled lots of our sessions because of the simple fact that he could not trap a bag of cement. And yet in a match situation he would just come alive. So we had to put up with all the negatives. He would wind us up but there was no getting away from his goals. Eventually we put him on a two-year deal. And then his form dipped through a basic lack of effort. That angered his team-mates and the supporters as well.

It all amounted to a real dilemma. I remember a board meeting at the end of Guy's first year and the directors asking me where our goals were going to come from. I told them they would be supplied by Guy – and they laughed because of the way he had finished the previous season. But I knew Guy would knuckle down again because his contract would be up the following year. He would start scoring goals again so that he could look for a better deal. And I was spot on. He couldn't stop scoring, in fact. That was when we had to try to get him out before he quit for nothing on a "Bosman" at the end of the season, as I was sure he would. Gillingham came in with a £25,000 offer for Ipoua and that gave us an opportunity to sign a replacement in Martin Carruthers, who joined us from

Southend. I knew Carruthers had goals in him and felt it was a good swap.

But, overall, promotion proved a step too far in these circumstances. The team had been weakened before we started at the higher level and it was a big disappointment to see us relegated back down to the basement again. Despite that, I had thought we would be good enough to stay up. The problem was that whenever we tried to strengthen the squad, the money being asked both for and by players was too much. This was Scunthorpe United. Along the way we had to use the loan market and did well to bring in goalkeeper Lionel Perez (later to play in the top flight for Sunderland) from Newcastle and Barnsley's Clint Marcelle, who had been one of the stars of their one-season climb to the Premier League. Those two gave us a big lift and we hoisted ourselves to halfway in the league at one point. Lionel was a great character on and off the field. He cut my training sessions in half! Lionel's philosophy was that quality was better than quantity. So if he made five good saves in training, that was him done. He had no desire to go on to six or seven; he'd just walk off and leave everyone scratching their heads. It was strange but he wasn't our player, that was the way he operated and we just had to accept it.

After Christmas we made further transfer break-throughs, bringing in striker Steve Torpey for a club record fee from Bristol City and signing Brian Quailey on a free from West Brom. But the damage had been done by then and we were not able to halt our slide to relegation. So much for the euphoria of 12 months earlier. Being back in the Third Division meant receiving less money from the Football League and resulted in more squeezing of an already tight budget. Every penny had to be accounted for.

It was against this background that I gave a trial to Gary Crosby, a former team-mate of mine at Nottingham Forest. He was struggling for a club and agreed to come training with us in pre-season. We played a friendly at Brigg Town where Gary did not do particularly well and I ended up telling him that I was sorry but could not make him an offer. There were no hard feelings. He took it very well and we shook hands in the car park. Just as Gary was getting into his car, some alarm bells jangled in my head and I had to stop him. I've mentioned already how money was tight at Scunthorpe. Maybe you hadn't realised just how tight. Neither had Gary.

"I need that tracksuit of ours that you're wearing," I told him as he prepared to drive away. Gary started laughing, he genuinely thought I was joking. In fact, I could not have been more serious. We only had two spare tracksuits for players on trial at Scunthorpe and I could not risk our supply going down by half.

Gary said he would send it back to us in the post, but I wasn't having any of that. I'd heard it before from other players. "I'm sorry but I need it now," I insisted. "I can't let you leave with it."

So poor Gary had to strip down to his underpants in the car park before setting off for home. I'm just pleased he didn't get pulled over by the police on the way. But that is the life and the reality of football in the lower divisions. Gary came to see the funny side and we've had a good laugh about this incident since then.

It was a similar story with Steve Guinan after we had brought him in on loan from Nottingham Forest. I had spent so long trying to recruit him that when I finally succeeded I wondered why I had bothered – because he messed me about. Steve agreed to stay with us for a second month but when the day arrived for him to sign the forms he had changed his mind and said he wanted to go back to the City Ground. I was fuming. He'd wasted my time and the club's time.

In an angry exchange in the car park, I told him: "If that's your attitude then off you go – but first give me back that tracksuit you're wearing." Steve wasn't very happy but he went to his car, stripped off and drove away.

When he got back to Forest he obviously complained about me because I got a phone call from them. But when I relayed what had happened they just burst out laughing. It was nothing on them. They knew it was just the sort of thing that Brian Clough would have done in his day. But this wasn't about me trying to emulate the great man. It was about necessity, pure and simple. We just could not afford to risk losing tracksuits.

Money was so scarce that at one board meeting there was a discussion about cutting back even further. I was even asked if I was aware how many paper drinking cups we were using down in the dressing room. I laughed at first but soon realised it was being put to me as a serious question. I was told we were getting through 500 of these cups a week. Now I don't know how much paper cups cost, but I am sure it's not a fortune. Nevertheless, this does highlight how clubs like Scunthorpe have to look at every penny they spend. I suppose one small amount multiplied by ten somewhere else does make a difference.

The day after this board meeting we had a reserve game at Glanford Park. My assistant, Russ Wilcox, was giving his team talk before kick-off as I walked in the dressing room and started counting the number of plastic cups on the tea trolley. I put them in piles and counted one hundred of them. "They're right," I thought. "That is a lot of cups."

Then I looked round and saw a player chewing on one – and I went mad. "What are you chewing a plastic up for?" I demanded. Then I shouted at somebody else, asking why he had two cups rather than one. You can imagine what the players must have been thinking. They were entitled to think I'd flipped.

Russ came across to me and said: "Gaffer, you've either gone stark raving bonkers or there's something annoying you." I told him it must be the former – so he suggested it would be better if I left. For all the funny side to this story, I can understand how serious it is when money is so tight that a club has to make cuts everywhere it can, no matter how small. Everything adds up in a big way.

Another area the club cut was the number of hours that the staff worked. Apart from people like me, of course! I think back to a game at York City on New Year's Day, 2003. It was decided that instead of going to a hotel for a pre-match meal we would eat something at the ground before we left for the relatively short trip to Bootham Crescent. But we did not have the staff to lay on a meal for everyone. So it was left to the groundsman, Graham Colby, my wife Jane and myself to prepare and serve the players beans on toast. I don't somehow think you would find Sir Alex Ferguson doing this sort of thing at Manchester United – or Terry Venables, then the manager of a Leeds United side we were due to face in the third round of the FA Cup just three days later. But at a lower league outfit everyone has to muck in together.

In the Premier League you'll find that clubs have a

squad within a squad, people who are there to look after the players and help the manager in his preparation for games. They have staff for everything, from dieticians to masseurs, to psychologists, defence coaches, midfield coaches, striker coaches, chief scouts and a lot of Red Indians. Lower down, a manager has to do so much of that work by himself and has only a small staff to help him. For instance, my scouting network at Scunthorpe was a group of friends I had put together to do the job for next to nothing. But a lot of the talent spotting I did myself. And whenever I went to games I would see the same bloody old faces of managers from the lower leagues all looking at the same games and the same players; all of us hoping to spot something that somebody else hadn't. Fat chance of that. There are few secrets in that regard because everyone knows the best players. It's more a question of whether you can afford them.

We're all gazing into the same shop window and it's not Harrods. With everyone looking on the same dusty shelves, getting that "bargain" all to yourself gets harder and harder. But it is still just about possible from time to time and even more satisfying for that. One dropped into my lap while I was away doing a management course at Warwick University. A coach there from Norwich City mentioned a lad called Paul Hayes for whom things were not working out at Carrow Road. We invited him for a trial in our reserves, where he impressed, and we agreed to take over the third year of his youth training contract. It cost us the princely sum of about £25 a week. We had a real bargain there. Paul looked like he had a decent future in the game and he has more than proved that, both at Scunthorpe and Barnsley.

Landing Hayes was just about being in the right place at the right time. But, of course, I have also had setbacks. I spoke to Crystal Palace about a quick striker called Steve Kabba before he went on loan to Grimsby and then joined Sheffield United. I knew he was a lad who could score goals but I got mixed messages from Selhurst Park. The manager, Trevor Francis, was telling me he did not want to sell Kabba – and yet Palace's chief executive was ringing my chairman saying that they would do a deal. To cut a long story short, I think I could have got Kabba for £50,000, which would have been good business. But we just didn't have that sort of money.

Another frustration you find is in trying to sign young players on loan from the Premier League. Their clubs will often agree to you taking them but then you find that the kids themselves don't want to drop down to the lower leagues. That's disappointing and I think it shows they have got their priorities wrong. It shouldn't matter to young lads what level they are playing; it's the chance of playing first-team football that should be most important to them, not least for the sake of their development.

Another cross we had to bear was that, for whatever reason, the name Scunthorpe seems to be one that people like to ridicule. Even I would be forced to admit that, at first, I didn't fancy the idea of living in the area, partly because I had been used to Nottingham which I found to be a fantastic place. But once I moved to Scunthorpe I grew to love it. And it's my family home to this day. I've stayed there while managing Sheffield Wednesday and Burnley and now consider myself to be a real Scunthonian. I like the place and I like the people.

It's still hard, though, to persuade people to join you

there. I found that with Peter Beagrie, my old mate from Middlesbrough, who went on to have a top career with the likes of Everton and Manchester City. It took a lot of persuasion and a lot of friendship to get Beags to Glanford Park. I remember one day ringing his home to talk to his wife Lynn and asking her what it would take to get Peter to sign for us. "Do I have to sleep with you?" I quipped. "I'm sorry," came the reply. "I'm just the baby-sitter!" Try digging yourself out of a hole like that!

Anyway, Peter did join us in the end to figure prominently in a team that secured my second promotion with Scunthorpe in 2005. His arrival highlighted the way there has been an improvement in quality in the lower leagues. When I arrived at Scunthorpe I never imagined we would see anybody of Peter's calibre take the field for us. He was a great influence on and off the pitch. I would always strive to improve my squad whatever the financial limitations. The day you stand still is the day you fail. I've always been one to try to re-educate myself; to get as much information as possible so that I could become a better manager and coach. That's why I went back to the classroom for the first time in many years to do the League Manager's Association's Diploma in Applied Management at Warwick. At first, it was a prospect that horrified me. After taking the course, I felt it was something that a modern day manager has to be prepared to do and it certainly carried the bonus of improving me as a person.

But there are still circumstances in football that no amount of schooling and education can prepare you to face. I can't close this chapter on Scunthorpe without recalling how I was effectively sacked and reinstated within the space of three weeks. These events occurred in

March, 2004, after Steve Wharton, a chairman I had always admired and who remains a friend to this day, honoured a promise. He said he would step down if we failed to get promoted. And that, sadly, was proving to be the case. Being a man of great integrity, Steve duly resigned and that was bad news for me. Even worse, as it proved, was the fact that a director called Chris Holland would be taking over.

I was in my fourth year at Scunthorpe. On the very first day of the Holland regime he said straight out to me: "You've been here too long!" It was as pointed as that. I'd won a promotion but we'd slipped back. Holland's intentions were clear and his thoughts were negative. He came out with a list of bad points at a board meeting. I suppose I didn't really need to be told the score but decided to bring matters to a head. "You don't really want me here, do you?" I asked. "No," came the flat reply. And we agreed immediately that I would leave.

My wife Jane was horrified. She worked at Glanford Park managing the club's study centre. "What're you doing?" she asked. But I still went ahead and settled severance terms because I didn't want to be somewhere I wasn't wanted. A certain stubbornness is part of my nature, always has been.

But Jane wasn't the only one to question my actions. Steve Wharton, who was still the club's major shareholder even if he was no longer chairman, rang me at home. He was equally upset that I'd agreed to walk away and asked me to explain my reasons. Afterwards, Steve said: "I'm not happy with this. Leave it with me."

I went away for a break with Steve telling me to sit tight. When I returned he rang to say that he would be taking control again and that Chris Holland was stepping down. The whole thing had got quite nasty. Naturally, I had no hesitation in returning with Steve back as chairman. We were struggling on the field and only stayed in the league by the skin of our teeth. There was more pressure to come because we really needed promotion the following season to justify all the upheaval behind the scenes. And I was as delighted for Steve as I was for myself that we duly got it.

Managing is about more than what happens on the field, though. I had a problem over a local lad at Scunthorpe called Matt Sparrow. He was a good player but always in trouble. Matt got caught on CCTV putting the boot in on somebody and ended up being jailed for three months in 2001. I had to go to court to give a character reference and I made a promise at that time to take Matt under my wing to keep him out of bother. But the court felt he had to pay the full penalty for his actions. That sentence would have finished many a young player and it could well have been the end of Matt. But we felt he had something worth persevering with. He served his time and then had to be tagged for a time, even on the field of play. But he had talent and he went on to prove it. There are people who can't reform but Matt realised he had been an idiot and I'm delighted to say the whole episode changed him for the better.

14

Safe Seat to Hot Seat: Surviving at Sheffield Wednesday

In every job bar the biggest in the game, there is always a time to move on. Assuming, that is, you are not moved on against your will! But, apart from that little reinstatement drama, I was never under that sort of pressure at Scunthorpe. Not that the club wasn't striving to go forward, far from it. The Iron and everyone associated with them can feel immensely proud of having climbed into the Championship, not once but twice. Sometimes I wonder if I might have been a part of that. Steve Wharton continued at the helm and he was a chairman I could always trust. It was better than a good relationship, it was a firm friendship. I think we could have carried on working together indefinitely. Besides, it was pretty much the side I left behind that won the first of those two promotions in 2006-07. And it was sparked by a couple of strikers I brought to the club, 30-goal Billy Sharp and his partner Andrew Keogh.

I also left behind some great friends at Glanford Park. Besides the chairman, there was a very supportive director called Simon Elliott who gave me a sponsored vehicle as the head of a car company. I became such big pals with Simon that I was best man at his wedding and he was best man at mine. His support for me – along with Steve's – was immense.

Nigel Adkins stepped up from his job of physio to manage the team after my departure in November, 2006 – and what an inspired appointment that proved to be. Nigel maintained the continuity and momentum that had built up from the second promotion of my reign. Hats off to Nigel. He then brought Scunthorpe back after they were relegated before leaving for a much bigger job at Southampton where he won promotion in his first season.

The decision Nigel faced in exiting Glanford Park was pretty similar to the one that confronted me before he took charge. You have to stretch yourself and to do that you have to take a gamble. For me, that meant swapping a safe, secure environment at Scunthorpe for one of the hottest seats in football.

Sheffield Wednesday had been chewing up and spitting out managers at the rate of nearly one a year. Relegated from the Premier League in 2000, they hit the slippery slope of spiralling debts as they floundered in the third tier. They won promotion in 2005 but were now struggling to make an impact in the Championship. I was hardly unaware of their plight. Apart from being one of our big brother neighbours just down the M18 from Scunthorpe, Wednesday were always a major topic of conversation in our household. My wife, Jane, was a big fan and so were many members of her family. She'd been indoctrinated by her father, Alan, her mum, Marie, and her brother, Steve, who were all huge Owls fans. Alan had a funny way of putting this into words. On the day of our wedding, Alan referred to my love for Jane as "losing a daughter but gaining a season ticket!" For me, the Hillsborough soap opera was a subject of only passing interest – until I suddenly landed a role right in the centre of it.

It was only in the approach to this momentous move that I immersed myself in the historical background. After Trevor Francis was sacked in 1995 – for the unpardonable crime of finishing 13th in the Premier League! – Hillsborough became the proverbial revolving door for managers. David Pleat, Ron Atkinson (for the second time), Danny Wilson, Paul Jewell, Peter Shreeves, Terry Yorath and Chris Turner had all been bundled through it. Now an eighth manager in nine years had perished. Paul Sturrock bit the bullet on October 19th, 2005, with the club fourth from bottom. So the next boss would be the ninth in nine years, if you follow my maths. There is a sense in which you wouldn't wish it on your worst enemy. But managers can be their own worst enemies when jobs like this come up. For so many, it becomes a fatal attraction.

Have you ever wondered why you always see big names linked with big clubs, even when they are going through hard times? It's because however far they have slipped, they have this special pulling power. In fact, you could even argue that the lower they fall, the greater the appeal. Not in a financial sense because even outfits with a name like Sheffield Wednesday have to scale down their wages, knowing that stretching too far is what got them into trouble in the first place. No, it's the challenge of being the one to turn things around, knowing that the potential is limitless if you do. And, of course, there has to be a bit of vanity involved, the self-belief to take it on. So, rather than running a mile in the opposite direction, you can find yourself going weak at the knees. I saw Wednesday as a sleeping giant with the potential to return to the top flight one day.

After nine years at Scunthorpe, I had served a long apprenticeship considering my earlier two years with Grimsby and I had to be alive to ways of advancing my career. Sure enough, some big names were linked with Wednesday. None were bigger than former England captain Bryan Robson who had enjoyed some managerial success with Middlesbrough. Also in the frame was Gary Megson, who seemed to have the perfect credentials having twice lifted West Brom into the Premier League. Megson also had the apparent advantage of being steeped in the Owls. His father, Don, captained the team in the 1960s before Gary flew the flag as a midfielder in the top flight. Nevertheless, I was also in the frame.

Steve Wharton phoned me one day to say that Wednesday had asked him if they could speak to me. Steve added that he didn't want to deprive me of the opportunity. He had always said he wouldn't stand in my way if a move was right. But he did serve me a warning. "Brian," he said. "Be careful. The finances at that club are in a mess. It won't be an easy job."

Of course, no job in football is ever simple. But some are harder than others and I had Steve's words ringing in my ears. I trusted his advice as well. It wasn't just a ploy to get me to stay. He was speaking as a friend. But naturally I couldn't resist finding out more about the job and confirmed that I would like to speak to Wednesday. I did feel there had to be something not right at the club. On the other hand, an opportunity to join a club with that stature and history – four times league champions, albeit a long time ago – was too good to refuse. And let me say here and now, I have no regrets about my eventual decision. Hillsborough was a wonderful learning curve for me and not without its rewards, not least achieving a spot of history and surviving longer than all the previous eight managers.

There was nothing rushed or forced about my joining Wednesday or their decision to appoint me. Actually, there was a gap of several weeks and that was very much in both our best interests. Sturrock had been popular with the fans there and his sacking sparked a demonstration against chairman Dave Allen. That was hardly a climate conducive to the unveiling of a new manager. But things began to settle down as results immediately improved with Sean McAuley, the club's academy head, in caretaker charge. It was against that background that I met chairman Allen and chief executive Kaven Walker. Not once, in fact, but three times. And these meetings lasted a fair few hours. They were very thorough on both sides. I wanted to know more about them as much as they were finding out about me.

I liked the chairman and the way he went about it. Dave Allen came across as a strong-willed character and he told things as they were, no messing about. Having worked so closely with Steve Wharton, I particularly wanted a relationship with him. In fact, my only regret about taking the job was that I couldn't take Steve with me. That's nothing against Dave Allen, by the way. He had his own reasons for preferring to keep a distance in the way we operated, much as I would have preferred to have dealt directly with him. When I mentioned that I would like a close working relationship, he said he felt he had got too close to Paul Sturrock and didn't want to do that again. Allen wanted me to operate in tandem with chief executive Walker instead. I had spoken to a lot of people who had warned me about the way Mr. Walker worked. But I like to take people at face value and find things out for myself. Which I did! To say it became a challenging relationship would be an understatement.

Another alarm bell was sounded in the press conference at my unveiling. We had agreed beforehand in principle on everything that would be said. Then the chairman remarked that ideally he wanted promotion within 18 months – that is, by the end of the following season – and that wasn't in the script! I remember looking across at him in surprise. But that was Dave, that was the way he was. It was in answer to a straight question and Dave would always give a straight answer. Besides, things started so well for me at Hillsborough that there was no way I could lower those expectations. The bigger the club, the higher the bar is set. That is a fact of life in football. We lifted the hopes of long-suffering fans by embarking on a tremendous run and eventually finished ninth, not far short of the play-offs.

There was huge optimism and I felt we would be in with a chance the following season – providing we kept our best players. Here's where those financial difficulties kicked in. Money drives issues for hard-up clubs when serious money appears on the table. The debt – and it was something around £25m at the time – dictates everything. Dave Allen took his duty to run the club in a businesslike fashion very seriously. Naturally, however, that wasn't necessarily in my favour with a promotion bid expected.

And that's exactly how and why managers find themselves forever swimming against the tide.

Our biggest loss that summer was Madjid Bougherra, a brilliant centre half and also a fantastic person. Bougherra had so much ability he could play in any position on the field. He was nicknamed "Magic" by the fans and it was easy to see why. Looking back, losing him was no mystery, either. Charlton came in with a £2.5m bid for a player who had cost the club £300,000 from Crewe. So, from the club's point of view, that was a tidy profit. But what put the tin hat on it for me was that we also sold another of our most influential players, goalscoring winger Chris Brunt. He fetched £3m in joining West Brom - where he went on to become a top player – just as my first full season was getting underway. Not only did Brunt hit the net regularly for us, he also provided more assists than any other player. Losing Brunt was a thunderbolt, a bit like one of his ferocious shots from distance. It was the start of things to come. Glenn Whelan, our midfield mainstay, left for Stoke in exchange for £500,000 the following January.

Looking at the way those three players have developed – Bougherra went on to join Glasgow Rangers – you have to wonder how different things might have been for Wednesday, and myself, with them in the side. Instead of the anticipated push for the play-offs, we ended up in a relegation scrap. I'll never forget our nightmare start to that season. There was depression around the place and we somehow contrived to lose all the first six games. Needless to say, there was speculation about my job ahead of a home game with Hull City on September 22nd. Thankfully, we won 1-0 to turn the tide and although Francis Jeffers scored a memorable goal, the big factor was bringing in two experienced players on loan, Graham Kavanagh and Michael Johnson. Funnily enough, Hull went on to win promotion to the Premier League that season.

Let's go back, though, to the events of the previous summer and the massive gamble I took in signing Jeffers. At the start of his career he was the bees knees, a gifted young striker who blossomed at Everton and then fetched £8m in a move to Arsenal in 2001. From there, it was downhill all the way, including his time at Hillsborough where he scored just five goals in 54 appearances. But people might be interested in the circumstances that led to me taking the plunge on Franny and why it looked a reasonable enough risk at the time. Having finished ninth in 2007, optimism was high and we just needed a goalscorer, always the most expensive item, to enhance the team. I had a meeting with Dave Allen and Kaven Walker, who were encouraging enough to ask me for not one target but three. But there was a price to be paid – I would have to release a good striker in Steve MacLean. His deal had expired and whereas most clubs would tie up their assets Sheffield Wednesday seemed to let contracts run down. They somehow thought it would then be easier to negotiate. Incredible!

I'd worked with Steve at Scunthorpe where he was with us on loan from Rangers . . . brilliant footballer, great awareness, excellent in front of goal. Okay, he wasn't blessed with pace, but 25 goals in his first season at Scunthorpe more than made up for that. He then became a legend for the fans at Hillsborough, helping the club escape League One. But he started to pick up injuries and that became a sticking point in my attempts to keep him. Kaven Walker thought he was a crock and that I had to release him if I wanted to bring in another forward.

So I handed in my list of three targets – Billy Sharp, who'd developed under me as a terrific goalscorer at Scunthorpe, and two Southampton players, Grzegorz Rasiak and Kenwyne Jones. Rasiak was the tall Pole – accurately described as a beanpole in appearance – with a lot of skill for a player of his size and a great scoring record. Jones had already established himself as a big hit with Hillsborough supporters by scoring seven goals in as many games during the promotion season of 2004-05. I was confident that any one of those three would get goals for me and give the team a huge lift. As established players in that position, they would all cost over a million quid. But chairman Allen said he'd get me one of the three – as long as MacLean was offloaded. I wanted to keep MacLean as well because you can never have too many quality strikers in my book. In the end the chairman gave in and said we could offer Steve a contract against his better judgment. But I still had Kaven Walker to reckon with and he wouldn't budge in the slightest.

That was the point when things were taken out of my hands. Contract negotiations were something I felt skilled at, the whole package, and I'd been doing it throughout my career as a manager. Dealing with players and agents was second nature to me. But Walker wasn't going to have any of that and I suppose, in fairness, it's become normal for control over transfers and contracts to be removed from the remit of managers, not necessarily for the better. Kaven felt I should simply set up meetings and hand over the negotiations to him. That's where the fun started. The offer made to MacLean was so lame that it was obvious he wouldn't accept it. Steve was gutted because he wanted to stay but my hands were tied and I lost him. But I felt the disappointment would be fleeting because I still had the promise of landing one of my top targets ringing in my ears. So I left all the talks with Kaven and concentrated on planning for pre-season. Weeks went by and I started to get anxious that nothing was happening. We reached a point where time was running out if we were to prepare properly. I'd always made a priority of getting deals done ahead of pre-season training so that new players could bond with the existing ones. There were talks with Sharp but Kaven felt the whole package involved would be too expensive. It was the same story with Jones and, although we could afford the fee for Rasiak, Walker felt his wage demands were too steep.

By this time I was well out of my comfort zone and not happy to say the least. What happened to the promise of pushing the boat out to get me a striker? We were losing MacLean against my wishes and not even getting anyone to replace him. Then I was summoned to Walker's office to be asked if I could find another striker to add to the list. With all the other approaches having fallen down, we were now in a mad scramble. Most, if not all, of the players worth having had been snapped up.

After much research, involving contact with other managers and chief scouts, the one name that crept cropping up was Francis Jeffers. So we set about talking to managers and players who had worked with Jeffers – and all the responses were positive. Yet all the stats told a different story. In fact, they were horrendous. After his big move to Arsenal, Franny made 18 appearances back on loan with Everton and didn't score once. He then managed just three goals in 20 at Charlton before another big fat zero from eight outings on loan at Rangers. And his record at current club Blackburn was 10 appearances and no goals. The only saving grace was four goals in nine loan games with Ipswich the previous season. Taken in the context of his poor injury record, it was perhaps not surprising that clubs were hardly queuing up to take Jeffers, even allowing for his undoubted ability and the fact he was still only 26.

But I felt he was a guy with something to prove, as was suggested by his recent successful time at Ipswich. We had to move quickly because, not surprisingly, Ipswich wanted to make his move there permanent. So it was over to Mr. Walker and the deal was done. I knew it was a gamble with Franny's record but thought that he was at the right age and we would see the best of him. In fact, he settled in very quickly and showed us all in training what a quality finisher he was and how his movement and awareness off the ball were exceptional. He formed a good partnership with Marcus Tudgay and all was going well ... until he got crunched by a challenge from Ryan Shawcross at Stoke. It was a crude tackle from behind and Franny was stretchered off with a dislocated ankle and ruptured tendons. I felt really sorry for the lad after all he had been through with injuries. He was looking every inch a top player and running Stoke ragged when Shawcross took him out. The injury sidelined Franny for the rest of the season and he never regained that sort of form in the end. In short, the signing was a disaster considering the wages we paid. But I maintain that Franny was very unlucky, as were we. It could have all been so different.

And so we return to the high point of Jeffers' time at Hillsborough, the vital goal he got for me against Hull to end a losing start to the 2007-08 season that threatened to cost me my job. Shortly afterwards, Dave Allen dropped a bombshell by resigning as chairman. There had been no hint of this during some pivotal discussions on my future a few days earlier. These, I should add, were not of a sinister nature, quite the reverse. My old club Burnley approached Wednesday asking if they could talk to me as a potential replacement for Steve Cotterill. Burnley phoned the club and did everything right, there was no attempt to go through the back door. They were refused permission and I then had a meeting with the chairman. I said I was happy to go along with their decision as long as everyone was singing from the same hymnsheet – in effect, that I had full support. Dave Allen quit a week later. It was sudden and the reasons were evidently rooted in the boardroom, but I was disillusioned. It's a grievous blow for any manager to lose the chairman who has appointed him. I was left feeling high and dry. No-one wanted to take control of the club at the time and we were a rudderless ship.

In the face of these difficulties there was a closing of ranks in the dressing room. We had to function independently, get on with our jobs and act professionally. It's at times like these that you realise how important it is to have a good assistant at your side. Russ Wilcox who has been with me in this role since 2000 has, throughout my management career, been a tower of strength and I consider myself fortunate to have found a great coach, man-manager, confidant and ally. He provides me with the absolute right blend of challenge and support and handles the role admirably. Not many people know me quite as well as Russ and although I may not have referred to him too often in this book, I owe him a great deal. Having someone to share your highs and lows with who completely understands the complex world of football, makes the life of a football manager much less solitary. I couldn't wish for a better right hand man.

For a time at Wednesday, when we had nobody but ourselves to turn to due to the instability in the boardroom, we kept our heads well above water. Then came one of those quirky spells when we couldn't win to save our lives. This was a run of eight matches without a victory late in the season. The fact that we drew the first seven made it even odder. On the surface it was hardly crisis form, but we were slipping slowly backwards. And when we lost 2-1 at Blackpool survival was touch-and-go. But we won both our last two matches in a dramatic and emotional finale to my first full season. A 3-1 victory at Leicester set up a crucial last game at home to Norwich. Even allowing for the club's smart move in reducing admission prices to gain us maximum support, the crowd that day was astonishing. We had over 36,000 in the ground and at first that seemed to have a nerve-shredding effect on the players. Norwich took the lead and could have scored more goals, but our lads recovered their composure to romp home 4-1. There was a mood almost of euphoria but it is seldom seemly to celebrate mere survival. My overwhelming emotion was the feeling of being completely and utterly drained. I had tried to relieve some tension in the build-up by quipping in the papers that my Owls-supporting wife would throw me out if we went down. Actually, I was only half-joking!

We were no strangers to big crowds that season and this is part of the appeal of managing a big club. The two Sheffield derbies stand out and these were a foretaste of things to come. More than 30,000 saw us beat United 2-0 at Hillsborough in January. Even more – 31, 760 – watched a thrilling 2-2 draw at Bramall Lane in April at a time when our status hung in the balance. Similar attendances would bear witness to our historic deeds of the 2008-09 season when Sheffield Wednesday did the double over their neighbours for the first time in 95 years. My Hillsborough job rival Bryan Robson was in charge of the Blades at that time. Steve Watson deftly scored the only goal of the game at Hillsborough in October before Marcus Tudgay, with a spectacular 25-yard effort, became the hero of our 2-1 triumph at Bramall Lane four months later. I was ecstatic to see this result written large across Sheffield derby folklore. We'd have swapped it for promotion, of course, but it wasn't a bad second prize. What a tremendous feeling it was, especially for someone who was married to an Owl.

My record in derbies was perhaps one of the reasons why I always had an excellent relationship with the Wednesday fans. I lost only one of five – a 3-2 defeat at Bramall Lane the following September in what proved to be the countdown to my demise. The supporters could see how much the rivalry meant to me and I think they also appreciated the fact that I always tried to be straight to them. Handling the Bonetti affair back at Grimsby taught me to deal in an even-handed way with the media and it is through journalists that you communicate with the crowd. And I have learned always to respect supporters. They pay their money and are entitled to their opinions, whether you agree with them or not.

So you can imagine my annoyance when there was an apparent attempt to rope me into some unprecedented legal actions that Wednesday mounted against some of their own fans at one stage of my reign. I still wonder at how I was almost dragged into that situation. I won't disclose the nuts and bolts but when I found out that I might be party to the action over some postings on a website I was furious. I demanded through the solicitors and Kaven Walker that my name be withdrawn. They didn't like it but my reputation was at stake. You can't have a manager suing his club's fans. It just doesn't work.

That said, I do believe the internet and fans forums have got out of hand. It's a licence to publish anything whether it's right or wrong. And yes, often it is libellous. Opinions are put out by people who remain anonymous and it seems they can say anything they like.

Unfortunately, the derby double wasn't the only stand-out episode of the 2008-09 season. In September we crashed to a 6-0 defeat at Reading. I make no excuses for that result and made none at the time. But there was an issue behind the scenes. As chief executive, Walker was very good at numbers and kept things very tight. But sometimes this was at the cost of results, in my opinion. We'd made a decent start before going to Reading and the exceptional nature of the result shows why I will always believe we should have stayed down there ahead of the game. A night in a hotel doesn't guarantee a good result but it does minimise the risk of a poor one. It would have cost us about £1,500 and Walker's refusal to allow it showed how tight things had become. We travelled on the day and got stuck in traffic for hours. There was no proper meal; we stopped in haste at a service station and grabbed anything we could. I'm not saying the result was all down to this, far from it. But it certainly didn't help. For me, it was a significant turning point – there was a huge fall-out between Kaven Walker and myself.

Without a chairman, Wednesday were going out of control. New investment was needed and there were no takers. I was working on a budget that was in the bottom four of the Championship and I felt, even on our good gates, we had to over-achieve to finish clear of trouble. Finally a new chairman arrived in the form of a supporter-businessman called Lee Strafford. In his enthusiasm, Lee put the cart before the horse. We had a budget meeting at which Lee said he was aiming to sell 25,000 season tickets. This, he reckoned, would increase the budget by £2m and allow us to compete for the play-offs.

But first we had to service out-of-contract players like Marcus Tudgay, Jermaine Johnson, Lee Grant, Mark Beevers and Tommy Spurr. They were our best players and a large portion of the extra money went there. That was on top of signing Darren Purse and Tommy Miller. Once I'd brought in those two players, Lee came back and said the budget increase wasn't £2m. It would be just over £1m. This was because his season-ticket target hadn't been hit. And that was really the downfall of that season. I've worked with a number of chairmen and Strafford was one on his own. He was very different. Primarily, he was a supporter and he came to engage too closely with other supporters on the internet. I don't think Lee ever slept. He was on the go all the time and I would get messages from him at one or two o'clock in the morning. I feel he was well-intentioned; he just got carried away.

My Hillsborough reign ended in December, 2010. We'd had a reasonable start to the season but nosedived in the Autumn. What struck me was that the players had given more than the maximum to perform against the odds and needed help. But I have no regrets about taking that job. I look back on it as one of the most exciting periods of my career. There is pride as well because I think it was a massive achievement in itself to have lasted just over three years as the club's longest-serving manager since Trevor Francis. We played some good football in that time, too, which was another reason I enjoyed a good relationship with the fans, and I sincerely look forward to the day when Sheffield Wednesday are back where they belong.

15

Parachuted into the Premiership

Who could have predicted that within a month of leaving Sheffield Wednesday I would be back in work? Certainly not me. Or that I would be managing in the Premier League for the first time? But I had strong links with Burnley, remember, and so the events that saw me take charge at Turf Moor – dramatic though they were – could have been more far-fetched. Burnley had closely examined my record at Sheffield Wednesday. They had figures to show that I had over-achieved with limited resources. I had a high return in points for pounds spent. Besides, life is full of surprises . . . more so in football than most other walks of life.

Take, for instance, the circumstances that saw me undertake a parachute jump during my time at Hillsborough. I still can't believe I've written that sentence. It was all in a very good cause, mind you, but the result of a rather rash promise. Not that I regret it one bit. The story unfolded after I took a call from a charity organiser from Sheffield Children's Hospital. At Sheffield Wednesday, we had close links with the hospital and the fundraiser told me about the plight of an 11-year-old boy from Scunthorpe called Daniel Grice. Daniel was in the hospital suffering from terminal leukaemia. Could I pay a visit to give him a lift?

We are lucky in football to be in a position where we are asked to do this sort of thing. It's a pleasure and a privilege and I've always been one to take such a responsibility seriously. So, as an ex-manager of Daniel's hometown club, I went along to see him. In the ward I picked him out straightaway. His pillow case and duvet cover had Scunthorpe United emblazoned all over. Daniel gave me this big smile when I walked in and we hit it off right away. For all the problems he had – which so sadly took his life not long afterwards – he had a real bright personality. I discovered that his illness had come to light after he'd played football and there was this bruise on his leg which wouldn't go. It turned his family's life upside down but they would always be at his bedside.

Daniel's big concern was to raise awareness of the disease in order to help others. He'd done a walk for the hospital charity and was trying to think of other ways of fundraising. Daniel and his dad came up with parachuting – and dared me to do a jump. Flippantly, I said yes. What else could I say? But it was tongue in cheek and I didn't think I'd hear any more about it. Then, a few weeks later, I received through the post an information pack for a jump at Hibaldstow airfield in Lincolnshire. One word popped out of my open mouth. I just went "fuck!" I couldn't not do it, could I? So I rang the parachute club to ask what was involved. They said I would be jumping from 15,000 feet – and not to worry, I didn't need to practice! "It'll all be right on the day," they said. I was totally out of my comfort zone. But they advertised the jump on the children's hospital website and raised over £10,000. Another reason why I had to go ahead.

All too quickly came the morning of the jump, which was in July, 2008. I've never been so nervous in my life. Puts even the prospect of playing in front of 100,000 people at Wembley or standing on a touchline in front of a baying mob in the shade. But it was only when I was going through the basics with an instructor that the reality hit me. I was to be flown to a great height and then jump out of a perfectly serviceable aircraft. Yes, I was! I hadn't taken in the reality of 15,000 feet until a few weeks earlier when, after the jump had been arranged, I was flying on holiday. There was a digital display of the flight details and when we got to 15,000 feet I had a look out of the window. We were above the clouds and I could barely see the ground. Bloody high! Bloody hell!

It was to be a tandem jump and I was strapped to one of these parachutist guys. There were just four hooks securing us together. I'd have preferred to have been behind him – let him hit the ground first. But, oh no, I was the front man. Up we went in a small plane which was very noisy. My partner tapped me on the shoulder and pointed out the altimeter in front of me. At 7,000 feet we were at cloud level. He indicated the reading again when we reached 12,000 and just said "get ready." But how do you prepare yourself for something like this? I was sweating profusely and my heart was thumping as we levelled off and the door was opened. Together, we shuffled to the opening. He said: "Right, lift your feet and cross your arms." He's still inside the plane and I'm just outside it. We seem to be an age suspended in that position. I'm thinking: "Go! Let's bloody do it!" Then we lean forward and hurtle down at

100 miles per hour. Panic. I can't feel the guy behind me. Is he still there? I think I'll scream but we're hurtling so fast that the only screaming is in my head. There's nothing coming out of my mouth because of the air rushing up into my face.

We were a minute in freefall and the only time I knew the other guy was still there was when the parachute opened. It had been the most frightening minute of my life. Talk about an adrenalin rush. When we landed safely I swear I could have lifted a car with my bare hands. I suppose it's why those adrenalin-junkie skydivers do it over and over again. But for me it was my first jump and my last.

The rewards were tremendous, though. Not least the fact that Daniel was there. Tragically, he died the following month. I'm just glad that he was able to see the fundraising idea in action. Sky were among television crews at the airfield and the jump can still be viewed on the internet. I've got nothing but admiration for Daniel. I'm in awe of people like him. He never thought about himself, only about his mum and dad. His attitude was so uplifting. I spoke at Daniel's funeral and still keep in touch with his family.

Only a month or so later I met up with another young kid from Scunthorpe facing a similar plight – James Neal, aged 13. I wasn't prepared to do another sky jump but I did try to change James's allegiance to Sheffield Wednesday and he came with us to a game. I didn't succeed as he stayed loyal to Scunthorpe. Very sadly, James died the following year and I did what I could to support his family. It's so important for players and managers to help where possible. We are looked up to as heroes and the effect we can have on people's lives is priceless.

And so to my Premiership adventure. Trouble is, there wasn't a parachute in sight. The timing wasn't the best, either, even though it was an exciting opportunity. I was drained physically and mentally at the end of my time with Sheffield Wednesday. I loved my time there but felt I had exhausted the players, too. I had wrung them dry with the squad we had; got as much out of them as I possibly could. We went nine games in which we managed a few draws but no wins. I still felt there were more than enough games for us to stay up. Yet my replacement, Alan Irvine, went on to have the same problem I had – no money. Anyway, I felt my time was up after a defeat at Leicester. If you can't change the players then it's easier to change the manager. I thought the feeling was mutual. I had a great rapport with the fans and wanted the club to stay in the Championship. I felt a new voice might help and there was enough time to get the team safe. It was a disappointment to me when they didn't stay up.

There was a positive for me in leaving. I was drained and could take my first break from the game in many years. I knew there was no easy route back but at least I could enjoy the rarity of spending Christmas with the family, thinking it would be no bad thing if I didn't return until the following season. Then again you can never pick and choose your opportunities in football; certainly not the timing. And a chance came up that would have been impossible to refuse. Remember at this point that it had always been my belief that I would have to take a team to the top flight in order to operate at the highest level. Here I was, losing my job at a club fighting relegation from the Championship and suddenly in the sights of a Premier League outfit . . . albeit, also one battling against the drop.

But while I accept that the move will have surprised people, the job is the same at whatever level you operate. It's about managing people and I had a lot of experience in this regard. I'd been a manager for 16 years up to that point and nobody could say I hadn't served my apprenticeship. Not only that, but I'd played at the top level.

What triggered my change of fortune was Owen Coyle's decision to leave Burnley for Bolton. Owen had taken Burnley to the Premiership in the first place and I completely understood his reasons for leaving. Beyond looking to advance his career, perhaps he'd taken the Clarets as far as it was possible to go at that time. But the fans didn't see it Owen's way. They felt he should have been 100% loyal and let him know that. I looked on wondering if Burnley's previous interest in me might be re-ignited. On the other hand, they were now in a higher league and my circumstances had changed as well. So I didn't think I was in with much of a shout.

That is, until I spoke with Brendan Flood, the Burnley director who is the club's main backer. Meeting Brendan changed my thoughts. He and the chairman, Barry Kilby, knew that it would be a tough job for anybody to keep Burnley up, especially after they had lost their hero manager. The club had the lowest budget in the Premier League by a mile but they knew that I could work within limited resources, as I had done at Hillsborough and elsewhere. Also fresh in their mind was that my Wednesday team had beaten Burnley twice during their promotion season, scoring eight goals in the process. They knew the kind of football I played, which was very much in line with Turf Moor traditions. It was an unusual one from the outside looking in, but considering my affinity with the club there was a natural fit. Brendan asked for my cv and then I got a call about taking the job. I had a great belief that I could do it and it wasn't just about staying up. If we dropped we had to be in a position to go again. And we did – only for me to lose my job at Burnley just over a year later. It still rankles with me as the most hurtful parting of my career . . .

16

In at Old Trafford . . . Out to a Bolted Boardroom Door

Looking back, the reasons why it was an unequal battle trying to keep Burnley in the Premier League are pretty obvious. Even at the time I went there, in mid-January 2010, the omens were stacking up against us. The team was competitively placed at third from bottom but hadn't won in the league for 10 games. Not that this could possibly be in my head when I took charge of my first game – at Old Trafford of all places! I had gone from one of the lowest feelings of my career in leaving Wednesday to an incredible high. Manchester United gave our club a refreshing reception and the Burnley supporters were superb. Okay, we lost 3-0. No surprise there, a respectable scoreline even. And I recall we played really well. We could even have taken the lead only for David Nugent, through on goal, to miss the target. That only served to wake up United who went straight down the other end and Wayne Rooney scored.

The Old Trafford experience apart, my eyes were wide open. It's become almost routine for promoted teams to have a good start, as Burnley had done. They were used to winning games and all the enthusiasm, the momentum they had built up, carried them forward. But the adrenalin surge only lasts for so long. These were not necessarily Premier League players. They were Championship players who had risen above their expectations. Eventually, there comes a stage when they are mentally drained and get demoralised. That's what happened to Burnley. There was also the shock to the players of losing Owen Coyle. They were close to him, as you would expect. I had no quick fix, but I did need to reorganise things behind the scenes. That proved the hardest part of the job. Owen had taken all his staff with him, there was no back-up and I also met with a certain resistance from the players. In a short time we had to bring in six new staff all the way down to a chief scout and a physio. And on top of that, the transfer window was about to shut. It was incredibly difficult, as you can imagine.

As is the way of the world, the media began to put my two win-less runs together – the nine games at Wednesday and the first four at Burnley, which were all defeats. This was totally unfair in my book. It certainly wasn't a losing streak. There had been some draws in my closing sequence at Hillsborough and some very narrow defeats in games that could have gone either way. For instance, in my penultimate game for Wednesday we had the better of a close game at Doncaster only for Billy Sharp – who else? – to pop up with a headed winner near the end. That was a cruel blow and the sort of thing that happens when you're having a difficult time. Another reason why I felt it was below the belt to put the Wednesday and Burnley stats together is that winning in the Premier League is especially hard at the best of times. But it was a great feeling to get my first victory for Burnley in the next game,

2-1 at home to West Ham on February 6th. I had almost forgotten how it felt to win. Beyond that, it was a case of winning over Owen's players and getting three points goes a long way towards that. Then they start to believe in your methods and your ethos. I felt it was important to keep a similar style and it remained pretty free-flowing. But it was also kamikaze stuff at times and I had to curtail that tendency. The team's desire to go forward was great, but their enthusiasm to get back and defend wasn't.

All things considered, it was a very tall order and our record of three wins at the back end of the season was better than that of other relegated clubs like Hull and Blackpool in similar circumstances. We were actually very close to surviving. The decider was away at Wigan. Had we won there, Wigan could have gone down. It's a very fine line. As for the reaction of the supporters, I wasn't their favoured choice when I took the job. Burnley's promotion to the Premier League had attracted a new breed of supporter and I was up against those. But they were willing to give me an opportunity, albeit a brief one. Their anger at Coyle's departure was bound to be channelled somewhere and it was me who copped for it. I didn't take it as personal, at least not at first. Beating Manchester United at Turf Moor early in the season had also changed expectancy levels. A team like Burnley might do that once in 100 meetings. Probably it was the worst thing that could have happened. The only way we were ever going to win was when every player on the park played to the absolute maximum. If one of them is off key, it's difficult. If it's two, you lose. So the task was almost impossible.

But we finished on a high with a 4-2 home win over Spurs in the last game. Harry Redknapp's side were looking for a top-four place and took an early two-goal lead. The response of our players in overturning it gave me great heart. It showed the fans that the players were with me. And the great lift from that result carried over into a board meeting on the way ahead. It was felt that if we could keep the squad together and add a couple with Championship experience we could bounce straight back. Everyone agreed that the minimum we should be looking at the following season was a place in the play-offs. Finishing in the top six was effectively my remit. I thought the supporters would go with me on that. Still, the mood was brittle enough for me to think: "God forbid if we lose two games on the bounce." But, in truth, we never did. And yet I was fired. Had we won what proved to be my last game – a defeat at home to Scunthorpe – we would have gone fourth in the table.

My future had become the subject of intense speculation ahead of the previous game at Barnsley. Those rumours were at the back of my mind. On top of that, Burnley had not won at Oakwell for 79 years. Talk about pressure! But I never showed it to the players. It turned into one of our best performances. Barnsley took the lead and people must have thought ' here we go.' The geography at Oakwell is not great for visiting managers – their fans are at the end which houses the dressing rooms. It was a long way at half-time with us trailing 1-0 and I got a lot of stick. This shocked me because we were actually playing well. I concentrated on working with the players who listened and we stepped up a gear to win deservedly 2-1. At the final whistle, instead of cheers, all I heard from our supporters was jeers. That was heartbreaking. It was almost as if they were disappointed we'd won. What true supporter goes to a game with that attitude? The whole situation beggared belief. It was surreal. That's when I thought: "We've got a problem here." The players got the same vibes. They were stunned. One of them said: "That's disgraceful. What's going on here."

It was against that bizarre background that I got a message from the board – a reassuring one – after the game. I received a text from chairman Kilby congratulating me on the win and saying it was a great achievement. He also said the board were right behind me. And so the scene shifts to Turf Moor for the visit of Scunthorpe two days later. The atmosphere was very poor and I could sense something wasn't right. I named the same team and prepared them as normal. But right from the first whistle, any mistake by a player was seized on by supporters as an opportunity to have a go at me. Let me tell you that any fan who thinks that booing will make a player better is having a laugh. In that climate, it's almost impossible to relax, enjoy the game and play your best.

Not surprisingly, we failed to get the win or even draw. Although we were sixth and still in a play-off spot, the Barnsley game had told me to watch out for my next defeat. Having lost 2-0, I knew the writing was on the wall but I followed my normal routine, which was always to go into the boardroom after a game. I got there only to find the door shut and locked. There was no-one there, they had all left. That certainly told me something even if I didn't know it already. The only people left were my family sitting in a corner waiting. We were all looking at each other, thinking 'something's going on here.' All I could do was get in the car and drive home. I knew that Kilby was away in America, so I tried to make contact with Brendan

Flood on the journey back. He didn't answer his phone or return my call. Another massive alarm bell. Other than the ringing inside my head, I heard nothing more that night.

It was the following day that I received a phone call, THE phone call. The man on the other end was Kilby, which surprised me considering he was away and not at the game. It was the shortest conversation you can imagine. If I said it only lasted a minute that would not be overstating the case. Kilby came straight to the point. "Look," he said. "There's no point beating about the bush. We'd like you to stand down."

I said: "I totally disagree. However, you've made your mind up. We'll talk when you get back."

We never spoke again. About an hour later, Burnley put out an announcement that I was leaving. I was disappointed both with the decision and the manner of it. I thought I had a better working relationship and understanding with the club than that. For all my love for the club over many years, this wasn't a pleasant experience. I can't dress it up any other way. The supporters upset me and I was dismayed at the way it ended from the club's point of view.

I did speak afterwards to Flood. I said we hadn't lost two games on the bounce all season. He replied that he hadn't known that. Brendan's reasoning was that if we lost again, the supporters would turn on the board. I thought they would have been stronger than that. Not many managers lose their job in that kind of position. We were on target for the play-offs.

Burnley then decided to bring in a very young manager in Eddie Howe from Bournemouth, where he had made a promising start in the job. No disrespect to Eddie – the youngest in the Football League when he was appointed by Bournemouth at 31 in 2009 – but the change didn't really have the desired effect. Burnley finished well short of the play-offs. Change doesn't necessarily equal progress and what was so galling for me was that the board could have been more supportive, especially as I was on target for our objective.

17

Management, Madness and Mayhem

Where do you start on this one? More to the point, where will it all end? People wonder all the time about the health of football managers, mental or otherwise. Why do we want to do the job in the first place and why do we keep on doing it? But very few stop to ask about the health of the game and the self-harm that results from boards of directors continually hiring and firing managers. One person who has asked that question is Dr. Sue Bridgewater. And she's done it in a very powerful way. Now Sue is the academic who heads up the business course for managers at the University of Warwick and, having done it myself, I'm a big fan of Sue – even though she supports Sunderland!

If Dr. Bridgewater's recent book, simply entitled *Football Management*, hasn't made the game stop and think then nothing will. In it, she compiles and highlights some shocking, horrendous statistics. Perhaps you've got a fair idea of these already but it'll do nobody any harm to trot out a few of them, least of all club directors. At the time Sue wrote, going on 900 managers had been chucked up in the air across a 17 year study period from 1992. It's now more than 1,000 in 20-odd years. Consider that for a moment –

it's like wiping out a small town or large village. Just as chilling, the average tenure of a manager has dropped to 18 months and falling. Often more than half of the 92 league clubs change their boss during the course of a season.

Of course, none of this seems to have impacted on the popularity of the game. Yet. The Premier League – where Sir Alex Ferguson remained, at the time of writing, the sole survivor since its inception in 1992 – is booming across the globe as the most popular football brand in the world. Brand? I hate that word – but there is no other way to describe the commercial success of the competition. The Championship, populated by many big clubs, has also shown an upturn. And here we go again. Re-branding under that name has helped. Meanwhile, the lower divisions keep chugging along, helped by the fact that clubs the size of Leeds, Nottingham Forest, Southampton and the two Sheffields, Wednesday and United, have dropped into their midst in recent years.

And yet Dr. Bridgewater suggests quite strongly that football will pay a price eventually for its insatisable chewing up and spitting out of managerial talent. Looking across the world of business in general, she concludes: "No sector could survive without damage the level of turbulence in football management and all the evidence from management suggests that nor does it improve the performance of organisations." I would add that there is a price to be paid in terms of credibility, although earlier in her book Sue counters this. "Football's 'sack race' seems to have become as much of a spectacle as the matches the manager presides over," she writes. And, hell, having known what it's like to be out of work after leaving Burnley, I suppose I should be grateful! You always know that possible opportunities are just around the corner. And I remember the ghoulish delight the media had over the trials and tribulations of my old mate Roy Keane while he was at Ipswich. Speculation about his impending fate was non-stop for months until he finally succumbed early in 2011. Even as a jobless boss, you don't wish that on anybody.

Casting all the emotion aside for a moment – and that's a difficult thing to do in this volatile game of ours – Dr. Bridgewater's wider point is made through statistics showing that, in the majority of cases, clubs suffer from changing managers too regularly. Rarely does it have the desired effect. But then this should be no surprise, just plain commonsense. As Sue points out in her book, "what would happen to our schools and businesses if half of them changed leader every year?" It certainly seems as if our game – for that is what it is ultimately – is divorced from normal professional practice. There have been some stunning examples of this in operation. Martin Allen was sacked after just four games as Leicester manager in 2007. A couple of years earlier, Steve Claridge was sent packing by Millwall before a game had been played that season.

Somehow football as a whole seems to be ignoring the most shining example that long-term success is best achieved by continuity. It is well documented that Sir Alex came close to the sack during his early years at Old Trafford, but Manchester United held their nerve and have been rewarded with an unparalleled era of success. There are other instances but they are few and far between. Most clubs just seem to make it up as they go along. Bristol Rovers and Dave Penney was a particular instance – he lasted less than two months during the 2010-11 campaign.

With this comes the expectation in the media that managers will perish if they don't get results from the off. It's easy to decry such speculation but it is football that has created the climate for it to become fair game. The question has been thrown at me more than a few times over my career and in most cases I've understood why, not taking it personally because that is the world we live in.

And let's be honest, nobody drags us kicking and screaming into management. Nobody throws us back into the saddle. We do it first and foremost because football is in our blood. It becomes a drug and we need that drip, drip, drip. Oh, and it's decently paid, sometimes lavishly so. Not necessarily at the lower levels, of course, but you see any job come up – any job, anywhere – and there will be scores of people after it. And the more managers and coaches who get thrown overboard prematurely, potentially wasted to the game, the more there will be competing for these positions. Precarious or not, we want to be involved.

No way am I put off, but I do think that clubs will keep going down the same dead-end route. It won't get any better, only worse. The job of management will get harder and harder – with less and less time to do it. I would even say it's getting to the stage where it's almost impossible to stay in one position more than a few years at most. Long-term success is achieved by only a tiny minority – and usually, let the game take note, because people have held firm during a sticky patch. But above all, there has to be a huge element of luck.

Where I wouldn't argue is that football has to be results based. It's quite simple; you've got to win games. But there has to be a period of preparation in order to achieve that – and this is what's disappeared. Don't forget that new managers usually get appointed when teams are struggling, you rarely inherit a winning team. Another simple reality is that, by the nature of the game, there are always more losers than winners over the course of a season. Only a limited number of teams can win championships, cups and promotions. What this all means is that the way managers approach the job has changed. It has had to.

Ideally, a new man would take time to get his feet under the table, as used to happen at one time. He would take a view of the club as a whole, analyse the youth system and the scouting structure, prepare a blueprint to rebuild the club over a period of years. Years! Now you can make that months or even weeks. So the manager will plough all his energies into what happens to the first team. He will look no further than the following Saturday and the result he needs to ensure he stays in the job. That might sound a bit dramatic but if you get off on the wrong foot with results there can be no coming back. A lot of potentially good careers are strangled at birth.

In my view, clubs should be run by managers from top to bottom. In reality, they have to neglect certain areas. You can get a situation where you need an experienced player or two to help you survive an early crisis. For financial reasons – and these are becoming more acute – you have to shift a few bodies in order to do it. So it won't matter to the manager if he has to unload a couple of promising lads who can become great assets if nurtured in the right way for a couple of seasons. No, expediency rules. Therefore, the talented boys get shunted on to accommodate an old hand who might get you a few results in the immediate future but who has a limited career span and no re-sale value. That's one example of why the shortsighted view taken by clubs can be absolute folly.

Driving all this, of course, is the impatience of fans. I don't think they have changed that much in themselves since I stood on the terraces at St. James's. They want their team to win and, having paid good money, are entitled to vent their feelings. What has altered is the climate all around them and I don't just mean in a football sense. We live in a world of instant gratification. Don't send a letter or make a phone call, just send a text or email. Want to see a film, simply download it. Need to know the answer to a question, ask Google. We can do almost anything – pay for something, sell something – at the press of a button without leaving the house. So when we venture out and pay to watch a football team we want good value – or else. If there's no entertainment on the field then a lot of fans will get their kicks by getting after the manager on message boards and phone-ins.

It's the world we live in and there's no turning back. Not that this is a whinge from an old stick-in-the-mud. Nobody has embraced new technology more than me. Computers, I-phones, laptops – I love it all. When it comes to football, a lot can be learned from the statistical breakdowns that give you information on things like completed passes from each individual player, number of shots and crosses, things like that. This can give you something the eye doesn't always see. So we have to use all the innovations for all they are worth. There is no bigger fan than me. I appreciated the way Sam Allardyce was ahead of his time in applying a form of football science to his success at Bolton. But this brings me to a negative side-effect of clubs being seen to over-achieve. Essentially, it's good for the game, fantastic when a minnow knocks a giant out of the FA Cup or, even better, climbs into the Premiership. But other managers often suffer by comparison.

Let me give you two examples. Burnley and Blackpool have both climbed into the top flight against all the odds in recent years. Both did it on relatively low budgets. Certainly, they were far from the big spenders of the Championship when they were promoted. So due credit goes here to Owen Coyle, my predecessor at Turf Moor, and Ian Holloway for the success of his homespun methods across at Bloomfield Road. What they did was great in that they offered encouragement to all similar-sized clubs. But this also created an expectation in boardrooms. "If Blackpool and Burnley can do it, so can we," they'd think. In turn, this would increase the pressure on managers, whether they were at a big club or not. Yes, promotion can be achieved on the cheap in certain circumstances. But what is certain is that it can't last without investment, as both those Lancashire clubs discovered.

Here, I have sympathy for directors, many of whom are well-intentioned and responsible. To a large degree, they are subject to the same pressures as managers – except that they usually stay in position without having to accept accountability for the hiring and firing. The least line of resistance when they are under pressure is to sack the manager. People are only human, I suppose. It's a vicious circle. And you can hardly blame boards for the financial restraint now being exercised at most clubs. Recession or no recession, it's not before time. For too long, football at all levels has lived beyond its means. But the fact that budgets are tightening across the board is another reason why clubs should be more sympathetic to managers and look to plan long-term.

Finally, I hasten to add that I am not tarring all directors with the same brush. Far from it. And I understand the burden they carry. There are times when managers run their course and a change is needed, sometimes for the benefit of all concerned. But here are a couple of examples of chairmen who deserve to be role models, especially in the current climate. Steve Gibson and Steve Wharton are people with their heart in the right place. Both are supporters of their clubs in every sense. Beyond that, and their considerable financial support, they have backed their managers at Middlesbrough and Scunthorpe with the gift of time over the years. It's priceless and it surely has to be the way forward for all of us in the game. Quite properly, there is increasingly more emphasis on clubs, particularly at the lower level, developing their own players. Yet this is the ball managers have had to take their eye off for the sake of self-preservation. So it stands to reason that it's in everyone's best interests to redefine the whole nature of the job.

18

I've Been so Busy How Did I Find the Time to Work?

I'm starting this final chapter in February, 2012. It's been 13 months since I left Burnley. By the time I sign off I could be back in management. That's the glorious unpredictability of football. You just never know what's around the next corner. I suppose 13 months is a long time "between jobs", as they say in the acting profession. But this is far from an unusual scenario in football in this day and age. There are a lot of good managers and coaches out there, itching to get back. But don't feel sorry for me, for heaven's sake. The time out has simply flown by, I've been that busy. For many out of work managers, it drags. They don't know what to do with themselves, lost without their football fix. I can well understand that because the game is a drug and I've been hooked since before I started a pro career all those years ago up in the North East. This is also far and away the longest time I've been out of it.

Yet, up to a point, I've found the diversion very refreshing. Invigorating, even. For a kick-off, I've got a young family second time around. And this time I've been able to enjoy the experience. Young Thomas is aged two-and-a-half as I write this. He's kept me fit from having to run after him all the time! There's nothing better than seeing a child smile and laugh. Thomas keeps our house warm and glowing. We couldn't be happier, Jane and me. It makes me realise what I missed with my other children, now adults. That's the price you pay when your job takes you all over the country – you are hardly ever at home. I'm also proud to call myself a grandad, by the way. Grandson Kai is aged two. I'm sure he and Thomas will grow up to be great friends – and you never know, they might even follow my footsteps by becoming footballers.

Not that I've taken my eye off the ball in the last year or so. I've travelled to watch games at all levels, visited clubs and done plenty of media work. A break like this allows you to reflect on your working practices – to review your coaching, leadership and management style. You can then take the benefits into your next job.

Then there is the fact that, as I've mentioned before, I'm a bit of a handyman. Give me a toolbox and I'll turn my hand to anything. And Jane is not slow in coming up with a list! So I get lost in various tasks around the house and garden. I've also been doing project management on a property in north Lincolnshire. That's kept me busy, too, and I've enjoyed all the banter with the builders. So I've simply had no time to be bored. There have even been moments when I've wondered how on earth I found the time to work. Then there's been this book, of course. Even that has been a discipline I've had to work hard to get into my schedule. Just as well, really, that I've been able to do it with the benefit of a pause for proper reflection.

Above all, I think it's important for people in any walk of life to have interests beyond their job. In football, that's particularly important because the game is so demanding on your time, so all-consuming. You literally eat, drink and sleep it. That is, if you can get any sleep! It's easy to become inward looking and frankly obsessed with the job. I think I'm fortunate to have a balanced nature that enables me to take joy in other things. And I feel the various education programmes in football for a life outside the game are becoming increasingly relevant. The terrible tales you hear from the lives of people like Paul Gascoigne and Dean Windass are a warning to the whole football community.

Okay, anyone in any job can suffer from depression. Footballers are treated enough as special cases without anyone feeling extra sorry for them. Why should they? In many instances, they are highly paid people who have done a job many others would gladly pay to do. And, of course, they should be able to look after their money well enough to safeguard their future. But, if you think about it for a minute, it's easy to see why footballers are more susceptible than most to booze, drug and gambling addictions. Not just footballers, either. Any top performer, be it in sport or entertainment generally.

All of us have our ups and downs. But the highs experienced by stars in any sphere are astronomical. Certainly, a good deal higher than the rest of society can imagine. It follows that the lows are much lower, too – right down to the deepest depths of despair. Of course, a player can experience this sort of thing quite routinely across the course of a career. There's no feeling better than winning, nothing worse than losing. But normally the two will balance each other out. Win one week, lose the next. And there's always that next game to look forward to.

Now try to imagine what happens when the curtain comes down; when there's no "next game." Most managers will tell you there is no substitute for playing; nothing fully replaces it. Being a manager or coach is just the next best thing. Then there is scouting, youth coaching or – and this is more lucrative than most management jobs at the top end – being a media pundit. But there is not enough room or jobs for everybody to stay in the game. The waifs and strays have to develop other interests, other careers. Many are successful at doing that and some combine it with being hospitality hosts at their local club, things like that. However, there will always be those who struggle to cope with what might be termed a normal life. It becomes abnormal for them. There are no highs and lows, just a long plateau stretching endlessly onwards. Where can they get their kicks? It's perhaps no wonder evil influences come into play.

This is not a plea for sympathy, just an alert for wider understanding. Let's suppose, for instance, you are a rock star. You go out and perform live in front of 100,000 people and millions on television. You have the national grid surging through you. Then you step off stage and wait three months for your next gig. Where does all that euphoria go to? And how deep is the trough into which it trickles away? Now think big league and European games, the FA Cup final at Wembley.

It's not just the top stars, though. A player can get a huge buzz from playing in front of only a few thousand people. He also knows what it's like to have the power surge switched off. He was somebody, now he is nobody. From being recognised and asked for autographs, he walks down a street unnoticed. It's easy to see how this can make someone question their worth as a person. Self-respect can disappear. I'm so lucky to be blessed with having a loving family around me and the mentality to cope with all the ups and downs.

Don't get me wrong. As I write this, I'm itching to get back into the saddle. Kicking and screaming, in fact. I believe I still have a lot to offer and things to prove. In fact, I'm a better manager now than I've ever been. Experience is a great thing, too easily discarded. I've managed at every level and feel that must count in my favour. Since I've been out, I have had offers – several in fact. But the timing and the circumstances weren't quite right. You have to balance your desire by taking a long hard look at the pitfalls. That said, there is truth in the old saying that absence makes the heart grow fonder. I've always had hunger for the game. Now I'm even hungrier for having this break.

One of the things I've done while out of the game has been to help stage a dinner in honour of Gary Parkinson at our former club, Middlesbrough. Many of you will have heard Gary's story. It's heart-rending but also truly inspirational. He befell a severe stroke in September, 2010, while working as Blackpool's head of youth development and, as a result, suffers from locked-in syndrome. He is aware of everything going on around him but is totally paralysed apart from the use of his eyes. At the dinner, Gary's wife Deborah spoke openly about the terrible situation he finds himself in and also of his fight and determination to keep going for his family's sake. Shortly after that came one of the most uplifting football stories I've ever read. Tony Mowbray, who played for Boro at the same time as Gary and myself, moved back to the Riverside as manager in October, 2010, a month after Gary suffered his stroke. Tony lifted the spirit of not only the Parkinsons but the whole football family by inviting Gary to help him run the rule over potential signings. Gary is able to watch DVDs at home and then communicate his thoughts to Deborah by blinking in response to what he's seen. You can't fail to admire Gary's spirit in the face of the most awful adversity and I wish him nothing but the best for the future.

Forgive the old cliché about things like that putting life into perspective. The reason it keeps getting used is because it's so true. There is always someone worse off. Luck plays a part in anybody's life and I've had bucket loads of it. I count myself incredibly fortunate. I've played at Wembley, I've played in the Premier League and I've managed at the top level, too. How lucky can you get? Hope you've enjoyed sharing the ride . . . so far!